40 DAYS TO A
HEALTHY HEART

A DAILY DEVOTIONAL
FOR PHYSICAL AND SPIRITUAL WHOLENESS

THANK YOU

With God all things are possible, including a Healthy Heart. This devotional could not have been written without the help of contributing author, Sami Kader, who started me on the path to physical health. He has provided in-depth knowledge and insight that has made living healthy a possibility for me, and has created an avenue for others to experience a Healthy Heart.

This book was an absolute team effort and though my name is on the cover, it took a village to make it happen. Thank you to Siobhan Oliver, my wife and partner, who labored with me both in writing this devotional, and in living it out. Of course, I have to say a special thank you to my parents, Rich and Lindy Oliver, for making me. Without them I would not be here, therefore, none of this would have been possible. And a thank you to our kids, Evan, Brigha, Meaghan, and Auston for wanting parents who can stay active with them.

Thank you to Kristine Dohner, an editing machine who brought spiritual insight, direction, clarification, brains and brawn to the project. A big thanks to Auston Oliver for being awesome, and for his amazing design work, and making it all (including the cover) look cool. Thank you, Jordan White, for being a health guinea pig, who helped kick start this whole thing by being willing to walk it this out with me. Thanks also goes out to Dennis Dohner, Kiley Oliver, Kelsey White, Tara Martzen-Byerly, Sarah Ivey, Sharon Bridgeman, and the entire staff for all their help, inspiration, and willingness to put up with long hours of talk about both physical and spiritual health. Last but certainly not least, massive thanks goes out to The Family Church and our community for being willing to partner with the challenge of being healthy and living with a Healthy Heart. Without you, it's just a book.

You Got This!

When it comes to exercise and nutrition, everyone has a different opinion of what we should or shouldn't be doing, how much weight we should or shouldn't lose, and how much we should or shouldn't eat each day. This book, 40 Days to a Healthy Heart doesn't attempt to tell us any of those things. For that reason, I could not endorse it more.

When I first met Matthew Oliver, I had been a trainer for over 10 years. He came into my life right as I started to feel a shift within myself. The passion I once had for helping people weigh in, make meal plans and stay accountable to exercise was quickly fading. After being obese as a child, weight loss had been my obsession and focus for many years. However, I began to see that no matter how many pounds I lost, or how pleased I became with my physical changes, I still could not see value in myself.

After repeated phone calls and endless messages from Matthew about wanting to get together, I realized this guy wasn't going to leave me alone! I didn't know what the catch was or why he wanted to meet, but I agreed to it anyway. After just a few meetings, Matthew saw something in me that I myself could not see. He saw greatness. More importantly, he saw what I was missing - value and belief in myself, and he committed to helping me find that value and belief.

Since we first connected, I have seen Matthew do this same thing for so many people - meet them, hear their story, listen to their dreams, then help them build a foundation to springboard them into their destiny. So when he shared with me his idea for a book to help people do just that, it came as no surprise to me.

As with any book, some portions you may relate to stronger than others, but the overlying truth in all of it is that EVERYBODY deserves to be healthy! Whether your goals are physical, mental, or spiritual, to get there you will need to take care of you, and give yourself the free gift that is health. The journey is not easy, but your dreams and goals are too important to go unaccomplished. I believe this book is a great tool to help you reach those dreams. There will be many challenges to face, but no matter what, never forget...You got this!

Sami Kader

Table Of Contents

Table Of Contents

Introduction

Growing up I was the short, chubby kid. I wasn't strong, fast, agile, bendable, or buff. I was just me. I never planned to be short or chubby, I just was. When I looked in the mirror, I saw: short and chubby, and assumed everyone else did as well. Children can be harsh. Even years later, I clearly remember the names they called me as a child, and some not-so-nice rhymes that included the name "Matt."

As I got older, I wasn't as short or as chubby, but my view of myself never changed. When I looked in the mirror I still saw short, chubby Matt - a view I let define me. It wasn't healthy, it wasn't good, and it wasn't even true. God wanted to change my distorted view, so that my inside matched my outside, but it was a process and I had to decide to let Him.

Over the years, I tried diets, running, going to the gym, and working out, but still felt like a short, chubby kid. It wasn't until I met Sami Kader that my view of myself began to change. At the time, Sami was working as a physical fitness instructor, but as I soon discovered, he was so much more than that. He introduced me to a few truths that have changed my life and transformed my view of myself. Truths that I want to share with everyone I come into contact with. Whether you are big, tall, skinny, strong, or short and chubby like I was, these truths hold the power to bring freedom into your life, and help you develop a Healthy Heart.

The second time we ever met, we were sitting in a Starbucks. Sami told me, "People need to stop hating themselves and start loving themselves. When we start loving ourselves, we start valuing ourselves. When we value ourselves, we take care of ourselves." My mind was blown. It was true. I had hated myself for far too long: the way I looked, the way I felt, and the way my body was shaped. It took a physical fitness instructor to help me finally understand what Bible School had never taught me, and what God had been saying to me all throughout the Bible. God loves me. All of me. The real me. Even the parts of me I don't love. I realized then that if I could learn to love me I could value me. In that value I began to experience the freedom to be healthy.

I remember asking Sami the best way to lose weight. Here he is in front of me, a fit, buff guy who obviously did not have a weight problem. I figured he should be able to help me with some simple steps. His response was not what I was expecting at all. He told me, "Matthew, you do not have a weight problem, you have a health problem." He explained that so often we gauge our health by our weight, when weight can be just one of many effects of an unhealthy lifestyle. He recommended that instead of focusing on trying to lose weight, I focus on having a Healthy Heart. I knew then that's what I wanted.

That day God awakened my need for a Healthy Heart - not just in my body, but in my spirit as well. Life flows from the heart; it is an important key to our ability to live life well. From the heart our emotions are birthed, our experiences are stored, and life is expressed. If my heart is not healthy, none of me is truly healthy. God longs for all of us to have a Healthy Heart.

A Healthy Heart is key to you being the best you. And, you being your best is necessary for the world around you to experience a great God through you. The question is: What exactly is a Healthy Heart and how do you get one?

The heart is written about a lot in the Bible. It says we are to love the Lord with all our heart; have a renewing of the heart; restore the heart; cleanse the heart; and keep our heart with all diligence (for out of it flow the issues of life.) The Hebrew word "lebab" describes the heart as not only a physical organ, but the source of all moral and spiritual functions, as well as the intellect and the will. In other words, the heart affects and encompasses the spirit, soul and body. So having a Healthy Heart requires being healthy in all three of those areas.

I have been a part of revival services where we have prayed for a mighty move of God to change us and fix the world. That sounds like a good prayer, but the reality is that a "move of God" isn't something God just does to us, without us. Rather, He desires to move with us and through us. Matthew 5:16 says, "Let your light so shine that they see your good deeds and glorify the Father." The intention is that when others see you, the whole you, they would see the glory of a great God.

God longs for us to be "complete, lacking nothing." In His goodness, He gave us everything we need to walk in victory, both physically and spiritually. He was willing to die on the cross, not just so we can have life, but so we can have abundant life. This is why your wholeness and health is so important. It's not only the key to our victory, but it is the key to our family's victory, and your community's victory. You having a Healthy Heart is the key to the world around you experiencing God's goodness.

We have all heard the saying "hurting people, hurt people." That is not only true, but it has been going on for far too long – both inside and outside the church. The opposite is true as well: healed people, heal people; joyful people, bring joy; restored people, restore; and healthy people, spread wholeness and health to others, both inward and outward.

Having strength and victory in your spiritual life, without building up your physical and emotional life leaves you unbalanced. I have seen spiritual powerhouses who pray for the sick and cast out demons, but are emotionally brought down by their weight or perceived physical appearance.

I have also ministered to those who appear physically fit, but are bound to a diet, pill, scale, or preconceived notion of how they are supposed to look. They are physically strong, but spiritually and emotionally stuck.

Romans 10:13 says, "They that call on the name of the Lord shall be saved." Our Christian walk starts with understanding our need for salvation. Salvation in Christ is the path for forgiveness of sins, redemption from an old life, and the birth of a life eternally partnered with Him. However, salvation is not just about a one-time prayer, it includes the journey to "work out" your salvation. (Philippians 2:12) The word for salvation used here is the Greek word "sozo," which means "saved, healed and delivered."

Many Christians believe in salvation for an eternal life after death, but not in the saving power of God for an abundant life, here and now. A Healthy Heart starts with salvation, but should not end there. If you allow your "saved" to stop with salvation, you may never lay hold of the reality of healing or deliverance in your life. Maybe you have experienced the miracle of healing: a physical healing, emotional healing, or a healing in relationship. Or, perhaps you have gone through some sort of deliverance. These are both part of your journey toward healing and wholeness in Christ. Growing in heart health strengthens you for deliverance from addiction, helps you overcome bad thought processes or lifestyles, and helps you hold onto emotional healing.

The idea of getting healthy sounds great, but the process of actually doing it can feel downright impossible. Don't let, "I have tried before" keep you from trying again. This will be different. The journey of *40 Days to a Healthy Heart* is NOT about losing weight. It's about getting healthy. It is true, if you want different outcome you will need to change your thinking. But change doesn't have to be painful, and it doesn't have to be hard.

Your journey to a Healthy Heart begins with the way you see yourself and the way you see God. Take a moment and begin with this truth: You Matter. God says so. Stop where you are right now and say, "I matter" three times, out loud. Do you feel it yet? You should start to feel a change. You have to know you matter. God loves you so much that He sent His son to die for you, to give you a fresh start, and He wants you to love yourself.

I can't stress enough that this is not a diet book. Most diets start with you hating the way you look or the way you feel. I was part of a diet plan once that said you can never start changing if you are happy with yourself. Talk about guilt! Good thing we serve a guilt-free God. He doesn't want you to hate yourself. In fact, God encourages you to love yourself, then to love others as you love yourself.

If you love yourself, you will begin to value what you do to yourself. You will value what you put into your body. You will value how you talk to yourself and treat yourself. If you love you, you will begin to take care of you. The more you love you, the more you will take care of you. Trying to make change out of self hatred does not work.

God wants you to love yourself, value yourself, and because of love, care for yourself. From that revelation, you may decide to do something, such as eliminate junk food - not because you are trying to lose weight, but because you value what you put into your body.

Having a Healthy Heart may also require you to change your view of God. Bible studies often focus on how much scripture can you read or memorize. God would rather you know His heart than memorize His words. When courting my wife, I wrote her over fifty letters and poems that expressed my love for her, my appreciation of her, and my desire to always be with her. She never memorized a single one of those letters. But on the "big day" we got married, she said "I do." She knew my heart and my love for her.

You can get so worried about the function of your relationship with Christ that you never truly slow down enough to enjoy Him. Without authentic relationship with God, you can only know Him conceptually, not intimately. I took my son out the other day for some father-son time. He asked me, "Dad, how long is this going to take?" When I didn't have an answer right away, he turned to me and said, "Dad, can't we hurry up spending time together?" That is how we sometimes feel about God. We know we need to spend time with Him, but can't we just speed up the process? There is no quick process to relationship or intimacy. It simply takes quality time spent together.

Over the next 40 days you will begin a journey. It is an opportunity to begin the habit of living with a Healthy Heart (seeing yourself as God sees you), ridding your life of bad habits, mindsets, or erroneous thought processes about God or Christian living, and beginning a life that includes being more active and healthy eating. It is the starting line, not the finish line. My goal is not to tell you what to eat, how far to run, or who to love or forgive. The goal of this devotional is to guide and encourage you to truly value yourself, so you will be free to make healthier choices in all areas of your life. My prayer is that by the end of this book, you will have a Healthy Heart.

How This Book Works

I am not a dietitian, a physician or a physical fitness expert. I am just a guy living life. I love food and am not that fond of physical exercise, but I do desire to be healthy. I love God, but found myself pressing into Him only in the easy areas, while avoiding the areas that were tough for me, like real forgiveness. Through my own journey, God has shown me some simple keys to a Healthy Heart that I now share with you. I have found many books that focus on getting healthier in one area of life, but few that encourage healthy lifestyle in spirit, soul and body. I believe God longs for that balance in our lives.

Having reached out to Sami Kader for input regarding fitness, I have incorporated tips I have learned from him over the years, as well as what God has been revealing to me personally. This is your book. Take what applies for you, leave what doesn't. When Sami and I discussed this book, he said that for many people the greatest thing they may do is just start. It doesn't even matter what you do. Being willing to do something may be more than you were doing before.

We all have different lives, goals and start lines, so results will look different for each one of us. If you look at the person next to you (your spouse, your pastor, or your friend) and try to compare your results with theirs, you may be disappointed or discouraged. You may see areas where they flourish, but you struggle, and feel you are not making progress. That is why you must know you are not competing against anyone. A healthy lifestyle is not a competition, it is a value system.

Establish and commit to your own personal goals at the onset. Perhaps your goal is to get more active, forgive more, eat cleaner or spend a little more time daily in conscious conversation with God. Knowing your personal goals helps you gauge your individual success and keeps you from feeling guilt that can come from comparing yourself to other people. I may be trying to run more each day, but running might not even be on your radar. Your goal may be for God to restore your identity, or teach you how to forgive. The choice is yours and God's.

God doesn't always deal with everything in our life all at once, or even in the order we think He should. In fact, what you see may not even be something He wants to deal with right now. It is important to take a moment right now,

15

pray, and ask God what He wants to heal, restore, or strengthen over the next 40 days. What is God saying to you about having a Healthy Heart?

During this devotional, take advantage of the Daily Challenges. Listed below is a brief description of the three daily action steps: "Say It" "Do It" and "Get It." You may not be in a place to take on all three portions of the Daily Challenge. That is okay. Be free. Achieving a Healthy Heart will be a day-by-day process of growth and development. This book may be a 40-day challenge, but you do not have to master it all within the first 40 days. It may take more than one time through the book to fully experience all the daily challenges. Or, you may go through the book several times and get something different each time. The goal is to stretch, grow, and develop a Healthy Heart.

Daily Challenges

Say It: The book of Luke tells us that out of the overflow of the heart the mouth speaks. James tells us our tongue has the power to build up or tear down. Our words hold power. They flow from our heart, which holds the key to our thinking and beliefs. You may find it easy to say hurtful things about yourself (the way you look, how you dress, your attitude and feelings), but difficult to find something good to say about yourself. The "Say It" challenge is a daily declaration for you to speak over yourself, your family, your destiny, your dreams, your passions and your desires. This is not something to whisper quietly under your breath, but to declare out loud. This is an opportunity for you to proclaim (to yourself and your circumstances) God's truth about you.

Get it: The song *Jesus Take the Wheel* was an amazing hit in the Christian culture. We all love the idea of Jesus taking over when we can no longer do something on our own. The truth is, Jesus doesn't want to just take your wheel - He gave it to you! One of the greatest battles to achieving a truly Healthy Heart is realizing you need to forgive, love, and trust. These begin with you and require faith, and self control. But be encouraged. When you feel you can no longer do it on your own, Jesus won't take the wheel from you, He will partner with you and help you through.

The "Get It" challenge deals with the "heart health" of your spiritual and emotional life, which affects your relationships, dreams, passions, walk with God, and even your health. Through each challenge, allow God to minister to you. When you cannot do it on your own, don't quit and don't back off. Instead, ask God to partner with you to help you develop a Healthy Heart.

16

Do It: First Corinthians tells us our body is a temple of the Holy Spirit. In fact, all throughout scripture we are reminded that our body matters. Jesus paid the ultimate price on the Cross for our healing and wholeness. Salvation is a free gift, but the state of our spiritual health is dependent first upon our decision, then our responsibility to journey in intimacy with Christ. In the same way, we are given personal responsibility to steward our physical health. The "Do It" portion of the Healthy Heart daily challenge is not as much about what to do, as it is to challenge you to do something. You get to determine how far you take the "Do It" challenge. I encourage you to be willing to take it further each time you read this book.

Disclaimer

We do not claim to be doctors, nutritionists, dietitians or physicians. The information in this book is merely our personal opinion and does not replace professional, medical, or nutritional advice. The reader should regularly consult a physician in matters relating to his/her health, particularly with respect to any symptoms that may require diagnosis or medical attention. The information provided within this book is for general informational purposes only. While we try to keep the information up-to-date and correct, there are no representations or warranties, expressed or implied, about the completeness, accuracy, reliability, suitability or availability with respect to the information, products, services, or related content contained in this book for any purpose. Any use of this information is at your own risk.

The methods described within this book are the author's personal thoughts. They are not intended to be a definitive set of instructions. This book contains information that is intended to help the readers be better informed consumers of health. Always consult your doctor for your individual needs. Before beginning any new exercise or health program it is recommended that you seek medical advice from your personal physician.

40 DAYS TO A HEALTHY HEART

A DAILY DEVOTIONAL
FOR PHYSICAL AND SPIRITUAL WHOLENESS

07-11-2017

Day 1 : START

"For every house is built by someone but the builder of all things is God."

Hebrews 3:4

"In the beginning, God..." That is how my Bible starts. God: creator of the universe; originator of all things. God started at the beginning. If it was a good place for God to start then it should be a good place for you and me to start.

Starting can be one of the most difficult things to do. I have sometimes quit before I even started, because the idea of starting seemed too difficult, whether it's to start forgiving, reading my Bible, daily devotions, eating right, or exercising. One of the reasons starting can be overwhelming is that we set unrealistic goals. God started with the heavens and the earth. He probably could have spoken all of Creation into existence with one word. He could have formed it all in one day. Instead, He took multiple days to create six days with a seventh day to rest.

Many Christians overwhelm themselves by trying to read the whole Bible in one sitting, then quit somewhere around Lamentations...if they get that far. When making dietary changes, they can go so "all in" they create a menu that leaves them starving, because there is so little they can eat. So they quit right away. Exercising is a great idea, but don't head out the door thinking you are going to run a marathon without ever running your first mile. Start at the beginning. Set realistic goals. Pace yourself. The next 40 days is an opportunity to shift your lifestyle into one of a Healthy Heart. This is just day One. This is just the beginning.

Take a moment right now and pray about where you are spiritually and physically as you begin this journey. Today begin with understanding that you are valuable.

> **"God started at the beginning. If it was a good place for God to start then it should be a pretty good place for you and me to start."**

22

Day 1 : START

SAY IT:

"I am valued. I am valuable. Today I choose to agree with my true identity as a child of the most-high God. I am called, I am chosen, and I am royalty. I matter. I break off any and all lies of the enemy over me that would steal my dreams, my passions, my calling and my destiny. I come into agreement with the value God speaks over me and who He says that I am. Today is not an accident, it has been given to me, and I have been equipped with everything that I need to walk in victory. Today is going to be a great day because I have been created for greatness!"

GET IT:

With most changes, starting is the hardest part. You can think about starting, want to start, consider starting, but until you make that first move, you haven't actually started. Today, take that first move. Start. Start today to value you. Break off any lie that says you don't matter, or that you are not worth it. Remind yourself that God loves you. In fact, He loves you so much He sent His son on your behalf. Start today by coming into agreement with God's truth that you are called, chosen, you are royalty. Do something today to show yourself that you value you.

DO IT:

There are seven days in the week and each day will have its own focus. Day 1 is Move. The idea of running 10 miles might be daunting or impossible, so don't start there. Start with moving: take a walk around the block. Make the decision today that during the next 40 days, every day, you are going to push yourself more physically than you have been. Watch and see what happens. You are on your way to a Healthy Heart.

SAY IT - GET IT - DO IT

Day 2 : WATER

"If anyone is thirsty let him come to Me and drink."
John 7:37

Thirsting is mentioned all throughout scripture and is part of our walk with God. Jesus calls us blessed when we thirst for righteousness, for we shall be filled. Thirsting is good, but it is also important to make sure we thirst for the right things. In the past, when I was thirsty, I loved to drink soda. I thought I was making a good decision when I choose diet soda. Sami Kader will tell you, soda is a bad idea. In fact, he has told me over and over again, "When you are thirsty, choose water." Our bodies know what water is; they are made up of almost 70% water. Soda contains chemical substitutes our bodies do not recognize and, therefore, do not know how to process.

As Christians, we may be spiritually thirsting all the time, but quenching that thirst with substitutes. We thirst for love and look to relationships. We thirst for purpose and look to our job. We thirst for value and look to our community. These substitutes can temporarily quench thirsts, but never truly satisfy, leaving us wanting for more. The goal is to learn to turn to Christ to satisfy these needs. Jesus told the woman at the well that anyone who comes to Him for a drink will never thirst again. When Christ is your joy, you don't go looking for joy elsewhere. When Christ is your peace, you won't need to go looking for more peace. When Christ is your love, His love completes you. A Healthy Heart comes from getting the water of life that truly satisfies, and that only comes from Christ.

Day 2 : WATER

SAY IT:

"Today Jesus, I thirst after Your righteousness in my life. Fill me up, restore and renew my heart and soul. Let your waters of life wash over me, refresh me and cleanse me today. I invite Your waters of love to penetrate any hardened area of my heart and bring new depths of joy. Today Lord, I declare that the waters of Heaven shall rain down in my life. I know that today is going to be a great day!"

GET IT:

What areas in your life need to experience refreshing joy, peace, hope, or patience? Perhaps it is in a relationship, or your workplace. Or, maybe you need a fresh revelation of creativity or ingenuity. Where have you allowed a substitute to try and fill the place where only God's refreshing waters can restore? Take a moment today and ask God to show you the dry and hardened places of your life that need to experience His refreshing waters.

DO IT:

Today is water time. This is an easy change that can be so transformational. Starting today, drink water. For some of us that is easy, for others that may be a challenge. Don't worry about any other health challenges, except to focus on drinking water. When you feel hungry, drink a glass of water. During a meal, drink some water. Between meals, drink some water. Make it a priority. See how many cups of water you can drink - try to get up to eight 8-ounce glasses each day. Today, begin to give your body the water it needs to truly achieve a Healthy Heart.

Day 3 : TACKLE THE IMPOSSIBLE

"For nothing will be impossible with God."

Luke 1:37

How many times have you dismissed a passion, desire, or goal because it seemed impossible? Things that seem impossible can quickly crush your drive and keep you from living your life to the fullest. That is why, when you feel you are facing the impossible, God reminds you that partnered with Him, nothing is impossible.

When my son was just six, he had a crush on a girl, 16 years old, in the youth group. Of course, that would be an impossible relationship, given the 10 year gap, and other obvious reasons. Did that stop my son from asking her if she would be his girlfriend? No way. Thankfully, the girl thought that he was adorable and just laughed it off. But in the face of what appeared logically impossible, given all the facts and reasons, nothing could sway his six-year-old heart.

A truly Healthy Heart gives you the boldness to propel yourself to places your fears would otherwise keep you from. Today, there are most likely things that are holding you back from pursuing your dreams or goals.

For the record, I am not a runner. For years, the idea of running, even one mile, was just crazy talk to me. Impossible! Then God challenged me, "What is holding you back?" It wasn't the road, the trail, or my running shoes. It was just the idea of running. I had never done it before, so I thought it couldn't be done. Nonetheless, God asked me to try. When I did, I found that it was possible. In fact, after a while, a mile didn't seem to be all that much, and five miles became a daily run. However, even after learning it was, in fact, possible, I still had to choose to do it. Just like we must choose to love, or forgive. He won't do it for me, but partnered with Christ, I can do anything. So can you!

A Healthy Heart stems from the place of knowing that in Christ all things are possible.

Day 3 : TACKLE THE IMPOSSIBLE

SAY IT:

"Today I break off the lie that says, 'I can't.' I come out of agreement with any thinking that says I am not able. Today I renew my mind; I put on the helmet of salvation that redeems my thinking, in Christ. In Him I am able to do all things. Nothing can hold me back or hinder me today from my dreams, my passions, my goals, or my calling. Today, I release the strength of Heaven into my life, as I step out in faith and walk in the greatness that I am called to."

GET IT:

You can do it. You can forgive. Forgiveness can be one of the toughest areas for us as Christians. Sometimes we are willing to love where we cannot forgive. Forgiveness is not only a powerful tool for our healing, but necessary for a Healthy Heart. It is a willingness to completely let go of your offense, and the right to that offense, even when someone has truly hurt you or wronged you. Let me say it again, you can do it, but you must choose. Today, ask God to search your heart and show you where there may be unforgiveness, or an offense you are holding onto. Then, no matter how impossible it seems, make the decision to forgive. Only then can you truly have a Healthy Heart.

DO IT:

Day 3 is a day to "stretch" yourself on purpose. Pulling a muscle during everyday activities is a common way you can hurt yourself. Stretching not only improves your health as it oxygenates your body and keeps your muscles pliable, it can also help you think clearly and focus better throughout the day. Some keys to remember when stretching: never force a stretch; always make your movements smooth, not jerky; don't lock your joints; and keep breathing during the stretch. Today's stretch is easy, a hamstring stretch. Stand with your feet together. Step your right foot back about two feet and slowly bend forward from your hip joint, keeping your back and both legs straight. Hold for 30 seconds, then switch sides.

SAY IT - GET IT - DO IT

Day 4 : BE INTENTIONAL

"Before I formed you in the womb I knew you, and before you were born I consecrated you; I appointed you a prophet to the nations."
Jeremiah 1:5

"Why am I even here?" I recently heard a gentleman ask while at the gym. I watched him from my treadmill as he walked from machine to machine. Aimlessly wandering the gym. Not much of a workout. When he left, an hour and a half later, he had not worked out on any of the equipment - but he went to the gym!

Similarly, just going to church does not heal you, and simply reading the words of your Bible does not set you free. I was once in a rough place in life and just needed to hear the voice of God. So I opened my Bible and let my finger land where it may. I could almost hear the chuckle of God as He whispered to my heart, "I don't work that way."

God was very intentional when He made you. Despite what it may feel like, you are not just a compilation of spare or leftover parts. The Creator of the Universe was intentional in His creation of you and all the intricacies that go into making you, you. Many want to get healed up and set free, but aimlessly wander "the gym" expecting results. It is the same mindset as those who want to love the world around them, but are waiting for someone who is worthy of that love. You can do the same thing in getting healthy: eat better one day, or work out at the gym one week, then expect to magically weigh 10 pounds less. Right. You can almost hear God chuckling, "It doesn't work that way."

You must be intentional. Change takes time, commitment and devotion. Be it physical or spiritual, your body deserves a purposed investment of health, exercise, and clean eating, which takes time, thought, and being intentional. The good news is if you make that investment, you are on your way to a Healthy Heart. Today is the day to begin to live intentionally.

Day 4 : BE INTENTIONAL

SAY IT:

"I thank God for today and the opportunities that lay before me. Today is a day filled with possibilities and my life an opportunity for God to display His greatness in and through me. Today I raise my expectations to supernatural realms and purpose to press into God's promises for me, my life, my family, my city, my dreams and my passions. I break off any distraction or discouragement that would keep me from focusing on the will of God for my life. I choose to walk in greater relationship with Christ today as I choose to live with a Healthy Heart."

GET IT:

You have to stop randomly hoping things will change and instead start purposing change in your life. God is love. It is the nature of who He is, a fruit of His spirit, and how people are supposed to know you as His child. It is not enough to just say that you love. Love requires action, being intentional. Today, choose to love, even if you don't know how. Make it a priority. Start with choosing to love you, then God, your family, friends, and those close to you. If you really want a challenge, try loving your neighbors. Or, go a step further and love your enemy.

DO IT:

Day 4 of the week is Food Day. Purposed, intentional exercise and regular, healthy eating always have results. Today, remove one unhealthy item from your diet for the rest of this 40-day devotional. Don't choose something you already don't eat, but something you know would be a sacrifice. Or, take it even further by partnering this decision with 15 minutes of daily exercise.

Day 5 : WHOLE BODY WORKOUT

*"I praise You, for I am fearfully and wonderfully made
Wonderful are Your works; my soul knows it very well."*
Psalm 139:14

The other day I went to the gym and there was a massive, muscular guy working out in front of me. He was one of those guys who had muscles on top of his muscles. He was huge. But when I stepped back, I noticed something funny: his legs were like toothpicks. It actually made me laugh out loud. It seemed he loved to work his upper body so much that he neglected Leg Day. Of those I know who work out regularly at the gym, I can't think of anyone who loves Leg Day. It is the worst. But you can't avoid Leg Day if you want a balanced workout. Those who do, look weird...and people notice.

It is the same for your spirit. I have met powerhouses who have prayed and seen supernatural healing miracles that blow me away, yet they struggle with the fundamentals of forgiveness and love. Paul tells us, in his letter to the Corinthians that if we don't have love, we have nothing. It can feel good to flex one muscle of the supernatural to hear the "oohs" and "ahhs" of the crowd around us, while being oblivious to the snickers at our "skinny legs" where we lack love or compassion. God cares about your total wellbeing: spiritual, emotional, and physical. He longs for you to grow in strength and stature using His gifts in every area of your life. He wants you to cultivate and develop the good fruit of His character and Spirit in your life.

Today is a good day to tackle the Leg Day of your life and develop a whole, Healthy Heart.

> **"God cares about your total wellbeing: spiritual, emotional, and physical."**

Day 5 : WHOLE BODY WORKOUT

SAY IT:

"Today I press into the fullness of Christ, manifested in every area of my life. I refuse to allow any area of my life to be kept from the redemptive and strengthening power of His love. I receive His joy, which is my strength, His mercy, which overwhelms me with kindness, and His peace which surpasses my understanding. I choose to walk in the truth of His love and display the greatness of His Majesty. Today I command every part of my life to reflect a great God."

GET IT:

Maybe the muscle you need to build up is generosity. Let God give you the heart of a cheerful giver. Many pray for the sick, have the faith to move mountains, but struggle with a lifestyle of giving in supernatural living. Today, talk with God about how to begin giving. Start by deciding to regularly give a tithe or financial gift somewhere. If you are part of a church fellowship, begin to bless them.

DO IT:

Yes, today is Leg Day. It is time to get your whole body workout into high gear. Leg Day means different things to different people. Today, take some time to focus on those legs, with lunges. Always remember to breathe. Keep your upper body straight, your shoulders back and relaxed, with your chin up. (Pick a point to stare at in front of you so you don't keep looking down.) Step forward with one leg, lowering your hips until both knees are bent at about a 90-degree angle. Bring that leg back to original position, then switch legs. Spending time developing your whole body will set you on your way to a Healthy Heart.

SAY IT - GET IT - DO IT

Day 6 : WHO GIVES YOU STRENGTH

"I can do all things through Christ who gives me Strength."
Philippians 4:13

Who is your strength? As Christians, we know our salvation is only through Christ. Through our belief in, and confession of Him, we have eternal life. A Healthy Heart realizes Christ gave us more than just eternal life. He gave us life to live abundantly, today. He is not only our strength and source for eternal living, but also for our daily living.

I have tried many times to do things or make things better in my own power and my own might. Trust me, making changes in your own power always takes more time, more energy, and often does not work out. As Christians, we know God is calling us to accomplish things that are supernatural so our lives can testify to His greatness. If you try to accomplish those things in your own power, you may wonder why you fail, or even blame God for placing the passion in you in the first place. God places those passions in you, not so He can do them for you, but so He can do them with you. He likes you and He likes doing things with you.

When my son was just learning to walk, I would hold his hands up and support him as he took each step. As he got stronger, he just held my fingers for guidance. It wasn't long before he ran everywhere. Even though he was now strong enough to walk and run, I still guided him when he first rode a bike, learned to swim, and stepped onto a skateboard. Every accomplished step led to the next opportunity to step out more, which required my strength and support.

God's intention is not to hold your hand as you only learn to take baby steps. God wants to guide you as you risk, believe, trust, step out with Him and get stronger, then risk more, step out more, and believe more. He desires you to press into Him as you grow and get stronger. When you realize that God is with you, cheering you on, guiding you, and being your strength, you have what you need to be on your way to a Healthy Heart.

Day 6 : WHO GIVES YOU STRENGTH

SAY IT:

"God, I need You in my life today. I need Your strength. I need You in my relationships, passions, dreams, family, and in my work place. I choose to partner with You as I pursue ideas, creativity, strategies and abundant living. I press into You for my strength, understanding that in my weakness You are strong. In any area of lack or weakness, I give You permission to strengthen and grow me in my belief. I declare that, because I am in You, today is going to be great!"

GET IT:

"I am all alone." This statement is not about being single. It reflects a feeling that says, "I am on my own." Aloneness can leave you overwhelmed and consumed by responsibility or the demands of daily living. Here is a truth for you today: you are never alone or on your own. That is a lie the enemy wants you to believe and live in. The truth is, when you feel overwhelmed, isolated and alone, Christ is there with you, partnering with you. He promises He will never leave you; He is your strength. For the rest of these 40 days, challenge yourself not to agree with the lie that says you are going at this alone. Choose daily to press into the companionship of Christ and allow Him to be your strength.

DO IT:

Today is all about strength, working those muscles. Whether you see them or not, you have muscles. Building muscle allows a run or walk to be more productive. Today we are going to do the simple, yet productive, pushup. Begin in straight pushup position, hands firmly on the ground, directly under your shoulders. Ground your toes into the floor to stabilize your lower half. (You can also do this on your knees.) Begin to lower your body, keeping your back flat and eyes focused about three feet in front of you, until your chest touches the floor. Push back up. Repeat as you get stronger.

SAY IT - GET IT - DO IT

Day 7 : DAY OF REST

"By the seventh day God had finished the work He had
been doing; so on the seventh day He rested from all His work."
Genesis 2:2

Our bodies were not designed to be pushed without proper time to
rest. It took talking to Sami Kader for me to truly understand the
value of rest. He explained that our bodies need times of rest to
heal, and be restored. That is part of the growing process, part of
getting healthy. If you keep on pushing without rest, eventually
your body will break down and weaken.

Scripture tells us that on the seventh day God rested, not because
He was tired, but because He had finished the work He was doing. I
see many who are looking to rest before they get healthy: looking for
a little play, a little relaxation, a little time to themself, before they
devote it to family, relationships, or spending time with God. They
are looking for time to rest before deciding to commit to a workout
or healthy eating. It is important to know rest does not mean break.
Resting is not breaking from commitments. We finished one week,
not the whole process. Today, as you rest in the Lord, don't break
from what you have committed to do. Instead, on this day of rest,
press into God and allow Him to restore you spiritually and
physically.

"It is important to know rest does not mean break."

34

Day 7 : DAY OF REST

SAY IT:

"God, today I choose to rest in You. I allow the healing waters of Your grace and goodness to wash over, restore, and renew me. I delight in You and the wonders of Your mercy. Thank You for blessing me abundantly and lavishing Your love upon me. Today I receive Your peace that surpasses my understanding and Your joy which gives me strength. Today is going to be a great day as I live greatly in You."

GET IT:

Isaiah 40:31 says that they that wait on the Lord shall renew their strength. The word "wait" in the Hebrew is "qavah" which means to eagerly look for, to seek, to desire. Often times we wait on God, waiting for Him to do something. But our renewed strength comes from seeking Him out. Today take extra time to press into God personally and seek Him out. You will find that a Healthy Heart follows encountering a good God.

DO IT:

Today is a day of resting, not quitting. Your body is healing from an amazing first week of starting, going further, and eating healthier. Today, give your body what it needs to gain strength and restore. In resting, don't just do nothing. Make sure to move, breathe, drink water, eat well and stay healthy. This is not a break from a Healthy Heart, but what your heart needs to be healthy.

SAY IT - GET IT - DO IT

Day 8 : THE POWER OF BELIEF

"Abram believed the LORD, and He credited it to him as righteousness."
Genesis 15:6

Belief is one of the most powerful tools we have as Christians. All throughout the Bible belief is mentioned. It is the gateway for our salvation, power for our righteousness, and our access to the supernatural. Belief can shift your thinking, transform your heart, fuel your imagination, open doors to creativity, and unlock possibilities.

That is why there is an all-out war on your beliefs. If your belief can free you, it can also hinder or hold you captive. How many things have you not done, not pursued, not attempted because you believed you couldn't? What have you grown up believing about yourself that has kept you from relationships, jobs, or passions?

Growing up, I always saw myself as the chubby kid. My belief in that allowed me to stay the chubby kid. It didn't matter what people told me, what I actually looked like, or what my friends (or even my wife) thought. In my mind, I was the chubby kid, so there was no point trying to be anything else. That is, until God got ahold of me. He had to break off the old thinking and beliefs that I had held onto regarding my identity. Once I gave God permission to change what I believed about me, it began to change what I believed about others. That brought me healing that allowed me to make better choices and live a healthier life. I began to believe more in myself, and in others. It opened the door for me to pursue friendships, personal dreams and passions that I had thought were out of reach. Today is a great day to be victorious in your belief.

"There is an all-out war on your beliefs."

Day 8 : POWER OF BELIEF

SAY IT:

"God, today I give You permission to search me and know me. If there is any area of me where what I believe is not from You, I ask You to heal it. I break off wrong thinking and ideas about myself, my family, my friends, my region, and even You, God. I come out of agreement with any lies I have spoken over me, my dreams, or my passions. I release Your truth over my life and I receive Your healing power into my heart. Today I will not be hindered; I choose to believe that today is going to be a great day."

GET IT:

What lie have you believed about you, your relationships, family, dreams or your passions? Take a moment to actually write them down. Then ask God what He believes. Write down His responses. Let His truth to replace the lies you have believed. Allow the power of His truth to set you free. Then, for the rest of these 40 days, refuse to believe any more lies about you, or those around you. Purpose to walk in His freedom.

DO IT:

Here we are on Day 8, a day to move. You have already made a choice to drink more water, cut out one unhealthy food, and stretch. Don't believe the lie that you have gone as far as you can go, that you can't push any farther or take any more. The truth is, your body greatly benefits from being challenged, stretched, pushed to the limits, and then pushed further. Today, challenge yourself to go a little further in your moving, walking, or running. If you move for 10 minutes, push it to 15. If you run one mile, try to run two. You will see that you are capable of so much more, and you are on your way to a Healthy Heart.

SAY IT - GET IT - DO IT

Day 9 : GROWING PAINS

"Practice these things, immerse yourself in them, so
that all may see your progress."
1 Timothy 4:15

Achieving a Healthy Heart requires moving from one place in life to another, which can cause shifting, developing, growing, as well as growing pains. In fact, it is impossible to go through life without ever experiencing discomfort caused by growth. It is in the middle of these growing pains - that time of blood, sweat, and tears - we often desire to quit.

Whenever I go running, mile two is the one that always gets me. It doesn't matter if I am running three miles or 10 miles, mile two always seems to be the toughest mental challenge. My legs ache, my body hurts, my breathing shortens... I am positive I am going to die. But I don't die! And, when I finally break through those (false) feelings, every time I push forward, I grow! I get stronger. I build endurance.

We experience spiritual growing pains as well. Trust is the powerful currency of love, and the key to a Healthy Heart. Unfortunately, the idea of trust can bring up growing pains: doubt, fear, and unbelief. It can involve risk and cause us to second guess ourselves and doubt those around us. Yet when we push through the pain that wants us to shrink back, we find we are stronger for it, and victorious for not quitting. You can never truly have a meaningful relationship with God, or those around you, without trust.

You can also struggle with pains as you grow in love, hope, forgiveness or patience. The powerful promise you can grab ahold of is this: growing pains are a sign that you are growing and may be closer than you think to a new season of strength. So push through! Today you are growing and strengthening your Healthy Heart.

Day 9 : GROWING PAINS

SAY IT:

"Today I will not give up or give in. Today I choose to press forward into the high calling on my life. I break off weariness and release God's grace. I break off tiredness and release God's strength. I break off doubt and release God's mercy. I celebrate that I am growing and getting stronger in the Lord. Today is going to be a great day because today was made for me!"

GET IT:

The Word says to trust in the Lord with all your heart, soul and mind. That is everything that you are. In what area do you struggle with trusting God? Take a moment and pray about it. Ask God why it's hard for you to trust Him in that area and write down His answer. Ask Him to heal those things that steal your trust. Today, make the decision that you are going to grow with God. Today is the day you are going to start trusting in Him.

DO IT:

When do you quit? You know what I am talking about. When do you allow yourself to stop? When do you choose to walk instead of run, turn back instead of pressing on, or take a pass day? Today is Water Day and we need to take it one step further. Don't stop. Don't quit. Water is necessary – a key to healthy living. Our bodies need it to run right, to heal and to grow. Try eliminating sugary drinks and diet drinks from your intake today and replace them with water. See how it makes you feel. Today, take your Healthy Heart to the next level.

SAY IT - GET IT - DO IT

Day 10 : THE TRUTH ABOUT TRUTH

"Set your minds on things above, not on earthly things."
Colossians 3:2

When I am working on getting healthy, I do not step on the scale. I don't weigh myself. I know others that check their weight daily, or even multiple times a day. Not me. Our bodies all react differently to getting healthy. Some days my body holds on to weight, while other days it lets go. If I weigh myself on a day that my body is holding on to weight, and I see that number on the scale, it can start my whole day off on a bad foot. The number on the scale may be accurate, but not the full truth about my weight, or a complete report about what is going on in my body.

God's truth is different than your feelings, but you can get the two mixed up. Because of that, you can step on the scale and allow that number to dictate your feelings for the whole day. God says, regardless of what the scale says, you are chosen, valued, and highly favored. His truth trumps any other truth that is trying to highjack your day.

Even when you are having a bad day, God is still in control. Having a bad moment, or a bad feeling, does not mean that God has abandoned you. Feelings lie. So it is important to live by God's truth, instead of by emotions and feelings. Remember, your truth and His truth can be very different. Your truth can be dictated by circumstances and surroundings; His truth is unchanging, life-giving, and leads to abundant life. The "scales" of life will try to say you are failing, not good enough, or that you cannot do it. They may include some facts about the moment, but they are not the truth of your life - not God's truth. His truth is higher than all other versions of truth. That is why a truly Healthy Heart can only come from pressing in to His truth for your life!

> ## "God's truth is different than your feelings, but you can get the two mixed up."

40

Day 10 : THE TRUTH ABOUT TRUTH

SAY IT:

"Today, God, I press in to the fullness of Your truth in my life. I give myself no permission to doubt. I break off any lie of fear, and I tell failure that it must leave. I break off any feelings of inadequacy or weakness and release the full truth of victorious living in God that brings strength and freedom in my life. Today I press fully into His peace, His goodness and His kindness in my life, as I choose to live a life that demonstrates His love. Today is going to be a great day because I am walking in greatness!"

GET IT:

What you believe about yourself is powerful enough to become a self-fulfilling prophecy. What God believes about you has even more power, when you choose to come into agreement with it. Today, take a moment and write down 10 positive truths that God believes about you. Throughout the day, choose to meditate upon those truths. That is how you live with a Healthy Heart.

DO IT:

No More. On Day 10 we saying, "No More Scale." Do not weigh yourself - from today through the end of this Healthy Heart devotional. For some that may be easy; for others it will be a challenge. Don't allow your day to be dictated by the scale. Instead, make good choices because they are good for you, and choose to live with a Healthy Heart.

Day 11 : JUNK FOOD LIVING

"If anyone destroys God's temple, God will destroy him.
For God's temple is holy, and you are that temple."
1 Corinthians 3:17

It is said that if a nuclear bomb were to hit or an apocalypse happen, the only food to survive would be Hostess Twinkies. These junk food snacks are made with unhealthy ingredients: artificial color, corn syrup, cellulose gum - even the ingredients that make up the artificial butter flavor are derived from petroleum. They absolutely have no nutritional value, but oh, they do taste good. Sweet to the tongue, those yellow sponge cakes, filled with white whipped cream...I can see you licking your lips already.

Junk food is designed in color and texture to hit all your sensory buttons that bring feelings of comfort and satisfaction. But it only lasts until the sugar crash. By the time a Twinky is actually digested, you are left feeling sluggish and sleepy, needing more sugar to prop you up, not to mention the unhealthy chemicals you just put in your body that erode your health. You can feed yourself with spiritual Twinkies as well. You can feed on a diet of lies, gossip, fear, regret and drama. Momentarily it can give you the feeling of importance, value, or preservation, but in the end it is detrimental to your relationships, family, and your relationship with God.

Feeding your mind a constant diet of negativity is harmful to your soul. Eliminating the junk you feed yourself is not about a diet, it is about a lifestyle. Physical, mental, or spiritual junk food doesn't just hurt you for a month, it can affect the rest of your life with detrimental effects you might not see for years. Clearing out the junk food from all areas of your life is important to truly having a Healthy Heart.

Day 11 : JUNK FOOD LIVING

SAY IT:

"Today, I break off the unhealthy diet of negativity, fear, regret, and the lies of the enemy. I no longer give power or value to junk food thinking in my life. I release the power of Christ to renew my mind and restore to me the joy of my salvation in Him. I press into the life-bringing resource of His Word as my daily bread. I invite that Word to lead me, guide me and fill me. Today is going to be a great day because today I am living in Christ."

GET IT:

Negativity is one of the worst junk foods that you can allow into your spiritual life. You may even find yourself defending it and fighting to keep it. Draw a line in the sand and say, "As of today, no more!" Clean this nasty junk food out of your spiritual cupboards. Starting today, and for the rest of this challenge, decide there will be no more negativity: not in your workplace, family, relationships, or church. Determine today that you will only feast on the healthy food of God's Word and promises.

DO IT:

Today is the day to clean Junk Foods out of the cupboards! It may sound hard, but you can do it! Starting today and for the rest of this challenge, clear your cupboard of any and all junk foods: chips, sweets, snacks and treats. It is time for healthy living. Choose today, and for the rest of this challenge, to remove all junk food from your diet and see that you will develop a Healthy Heart.

SAY IT - GET IT - DO IT

Day 12 : NO PAIN, NO GAIN

"For to me, to live is Christ and to die is gain."
Philippians 1:21

When you go to a gym, you don't expect trainers to tell you that you are in such good shape you don't need to work out. You don't expect them to say "Why are you here? You already look good in those workout clothes." Instead, you give them permission to tell you what you need to hear, the tough truths, and to challenge you to get better. Conversely, many Christians do come to church wanting only to hear that they are so good they don't need a spiritual workout. They think: "Don't challenge me." "Don't make me uncomfortable." "Make this quick and easy and let me get out of here." Yet they expect change. When that doesn't happen, often they blame the church, the service, the message, or the music. To truly grow, there must be a willingness to admit there needs to be change and an openness to hear it.

Our Christian walk, much like our physical walk, requires us to be willing to face tough truths about ourselves and be vulnerable with God. For spiritual health we must be willing to ask hard questions about any area of our spiritual walk where we have become lax or lazy. We must be willing to face the answers, and then do something about it.

Holy Spirit may already be speaking to you about areas you have known you need to address, but have not yet been willing to. Those things won't keep you from going to Heaven, but they can keep you from a Healthy Heart. It is the same for us physically. Going to the gym knowing what exercises you need to do is not the same as actually doing them. A Healthy Heart is willing to accept the challenge to be healthy.

Day 12 : NO PAIN, NO GAIN

SAY IT:

"Today I release God's truth into my life. I lay hold of the truth that truly sets me free. I declare that I am free today to pursue who I really am in Christ. As a mighty child of God, I accept the challenge to have a Healthy Heart, and I release the fullness of an awesome destiny into my life. I refuse to allow any challenges of today keep me back or hinder me from my high calling. I am ready to face the challenge of this day. Today is going to be great!"

GET IT:

What is an area that you have been avoiding in your life? What is that sore area Holy Spirit has been speaking to you about, but you haven't been willing to deal with? Perhaps it involves unforgiveness, bitterness, addiction, or anger. Today is a great day to get real, honest, and willing to deal with the painful stuff. Ask God to help you and show you where to start. Then do it. When you do, you are on your way to a Healthy Heart.

DO IT:

Alright, what physical challenge have you been avoiding? Pull ups, sit ups, down ups, anything with the word "up"? Today is a good day for Up. The thing I hate more than anything else is stairs or "step ups." On this Leg Day I challenge you to find a good flight of stairs, in a mall, office building, or your apartment complex, and go up and down them for at least five minutes. It may be painful, you will feel it, but when you conquer it, you will be on your way to a Healthy Heart.

SAY IT - GET IT - DO IT

Day 13 : STOP NEGATIVITY

"For My thoughts are not your thoughts, nor are your ways My ways,"
declares the Lord. "For as the heavens are higher than the earth, so
are My ways higher than your ways and My thoughts than your thoughts."
Isaiah 55:8

"You Got This!" The first time I heard Sami Kader yell those words at me was at the end of a 30 minute circuit training. Sweat was pouring from my brow, my legs felt like bags of sand, and my arms could barely move. I hurt all over. I had every reason to quit, every reason to stop and walk (or crawl) away. I didn't feel good, didn't look good, and I didn't want to be there anymore. Yet when someone tells you that you can do it, even when you feel like you can't, it does something to you. Those little words "you can do it" release potential and possibility you didn't even know you had.

Negativity is a hope killer, a faith killer, a Healthy Heart killer. I talked with a friend once who said, "I am not being negative, I am being realistic." As Christians, our reality should not defined by what we see, what we feel or how we feel. Our reality is defined by the Truth of Christ and the revelation of who He is in and through us. Christ, who despite all the evidence of reality (what was and was not possible), rose from the grave. Despite what everyone knew to be true up until that point, He conquered death and redefined reality.

Christ's victory over death alone is a reason to celebrate and be positive every day in your workplace, relationships, and family, you get to decide which reality you will believe - negative or positive. When you face impossible situations that look bad, feel bad, or cause you to question your ability to stand strong or advance, God is rooting you on. Your Heavenly Father is encouraging, "You Got This!" He made the way for you to walk in victory with a Healthy Heart that does not back down, but lays hold of victory today!

Day 13 : STOP NEGATIVITY

SAY IT:
"Today, Lord, I demolish every argument and pretense that sets itself up against the knowledge of who You are, and who I am in You. I take captive every thought and make it obedient to the truth of Christ. I choose to believe Your promises about me, my family, my dreams and my destiny. I break off any doubt and negativity as I walk in the reality of Your presence in my life. Today is going to be a great day because today I choose greatness!"

GET IT:
Negativity is a cancer to the soul. It consumes all areas of life around it and can lead to isolation and depression. It is a dark cloud that can consume your passions and dreams, and kill relationships. Pray and ask yourself where you may have allowed negativity to take residence in your life, relationships, or dreams. Take a moment and allow God to heal and set you free from the things he shows you. A Healthy Heart comes from knowing "You Got This!"

DO IT:
What have you been avoiding because you don't think you can do it? By now you are already drinking water, moving more, and you have cleaned out the junk food. But what have you been avoiding? For me it's sit-ups. Today's Muscle Day challenge is to take 10 minutes and do some sit-ups: standard, crunches, or bicycle style. As you work that core, remember, "You Got This!"

SAY IT - GET IT - DO IT

Day 14 : SET, GOAL, SCORE!

"A man's heart plans his way, But the Lord directs his steps."

Proverbs 16:9

"No one plans to fail, they fail to plan." My dad has told me that for years. When my son plays soccer, he loves to score a goal. Who doesn't? You can hear the crowd roar, feel the energy, sense the victory. My son told me, "Sometimes you can get a goal by accident, but most of the time it requires a plan, and a lot of practice." That doesn't just apply to sports.

I am sure you haven't come this far toward a Healthy Heart just to give up or lose. But do you have to plan to succeed? The problem with most diets is that once they are finished, we go right back to the lifestyle we had before: same old habits, eating, and lack of exercise. We do this internally as well. When I talk to people who struggle with addiction, the first thing I ask is if they really want freedom. If we really want freedom, we have to set up a plan to succeed. Recently, my wife and I had been doing a cleanse that required no sugar. Yet my wife had a box of Thornton chocolates in the refrigerator she was saving. Every day she would sneak one chocolate. One day she confessed this to me. I told her the way to deal with it was to just throw the box of chocolates away. "No!" She cried out. Why? She didn't want to get rid of the chocolates. She enjoyed that little treat.

Some of us really don't want to change and we don't have a plan to change, because we enjoy our food, our TV, or our gossip too much. Unfortunately, nothing changes until something changes. Are you willing to really change? If so, are you willing to make a plan and set a goal? Create a plan today for a Healthy Heart.

"Do you have a plan to succeed?"

48

Day 14 : SET, GOAL, SCORE!

SAY IT:
"Today I break off distractions that would try to keep me from my destiny in Christ. I choose to renew my mind with the focus and the clarity of His promises and His Word that is living in me. I release strategies, ideas, creativity and heavenly downloads into my life, dreams and destiny. Today is going to be a great day because I am equipped to live greatly."

GET IT:
Our words hold the power to speak life or death. They can build up, or they can tear down. Your words are powerful enough to unlock potential in you and those around you. Today make it a goal (something that you are going to intentionally work on) to speak praise and positive statements over those around you. Find something positive and uplifting about someone, then encourage them. You will quickly see that positivity creates in you a Healthy Heart.

DO IT:
Goals help us determine our success. They help us gauge our progress. At the start of this devotional you were challenged to make a goal. Did you do it? How are you doing on your goal? Maybe your physical goal was to walk every day, or run every day, to go one mile, or two. By now you may find that you have done it easily, or perhaps missed the mark all together. Today, on this Rest Day, take a moment, update your goal and set a plan to achieve it.

SAY IT - GET IT - DO IT

Day 15 : MOVE

"For in Him we live and move and have our being."
Acts 17:28

I have children, so I hear the word "move" all of the time. Usually it is in the context of "move out of my way," or "would you just move?" Most of us have heard those words at some time in our life, maybe a provoking response to a stationary moment in life. Yet when we choose to move, to change our position or to take action, it can be one of the most powerful decisions we make. The command to "move" has a negative connotation, but the voluntary action of moving can set our heart in the right direction.

There may be places in your life where you have settled because nothing has forced you to move. It could be a relationship that is toxic, a friendship that brings you down, unforgiveness that creates bitterness, or anger that is fueling division. If you haven't been forced to move out of agreement with these things, you will likely stay. Today is a day to move, to make a change, to take action.

Even our relationship with God should have movement. He longs for us to seek Him and to reach out to Him for strength every day. He will never force this upon us. God, in all of His infinite power and wisdom, does not make us seek Him. He invites us to partner with Him in every area of our daily lives, but gives us the freedom to choose. Today, choose to move closer to God. It is part of having a Healthy Heart.

Day 15 : MOVE

SAY IT:

"Today, God I choose You. I pursue You in my life, my heart, my passions and my dreams. I come out of agreement with those things that keep me stuck in my attitude or my heart. I voluntarily choose to follow You and partner with You in all areas of my life. Today is going to be a great day because today I release the movement of Heaven in my life."

GET IT:

Stuck areas of thinking - that is what my father has called it. It refers to those places of attitude or mindset from which we cannot move past, or even forward. These are places where we get stubborn in our resolve to do it on our own. Where have you been trying to do it on your own? Is it working? With God, would it be better? God will not force you to need Him; He is good and loving. It is when you choose, voluntarily, to seek Him and move toward Him that He will meet and partner with you toward a Healthy Heart. Choose today to take action and move toward the Lord.

DO IT:

Today is all about move: it is a Get Up and Move Day. Make it a point today to move, to get out and walk, run, or bike. Fitness guidelines recommend you walk 10,000 steps in an average day. Most smart phones come equipped with an app to track this for you. So today, on Get Up and Move Day, try to get in your 10,000 steps. You are on your way to a Healthy Heart.

SAY IT - GET IT - DO IT

Day 16 : SHOW UP

"I raised you up for this very purpose, that I might display my power
in you and that My name might be proclaimed in all the earth."
Romans 9:17

For a season in my life I attended circuit training classes, twice a week. One day, a younger guy I had never seen before, showed up to class. He came in eager and excited. His performance was amazing. He owned every exercise with excellence. Then the trainer opened the side door and had us run around the building. This young kid came in first place, and lapped us all. Then, he was gone. That was it, never saw him again. I asked the trainer where he went. He said from time to time, someone will randomly wander in and get burned out in the first class. He said "they show off when they just need to show up."

This young guy had enough energy for one time, but not enough to be consistent. How many times in my life have I showed off when I just needed to show up? Life is not lived in one day, but day after day after day. My dad told me, "In life, talent will get you there, but character will keep you there." Do you have the character to show up every day of your life, for life?

There have been times in my relationships when I have showed off where God just called me to show up. In the same way, Christianity has less to do with what happens on a stage during a service, and more to do with what happens on a Monday morning...or a Tuesday afternoon. Victorious Christian living was never meant to be a one-time event, where we flex our spiritual muscles and lap everyone else, but a day-after-day relationship where we continue to fall more in love with Jesus. A Healthy Heart comes from showing up and allowing God to show off in our life.

Day 16 : SHOW UP

SAY IT:

"Today I declare the goodness and greatness of my awesome God. I thank You for the opportunity to fall more in love with You today. I break off any area of pride or arrogance in my heart, and humble myself before Your majesty. Today, I will show up in my friendships, family relationships, workplace, dreams, destiny, and in my journey with you, God. Because I am in Christ, I am expectant today is going to be a great day."

GET IT:

You can be in a relationship with Christ and not be active, or not "show up." The challenge today is to be present in your relationship with Christ. Take a moment, pray and ask God how you can be more active in your relationship with Him today. Ask God, "How can I partner with You today in living greatly, abundantly and as a testimony to You?" Then do it. That is the true challenge to a Healthy Heart.

DO IT:

We can all push ourselves once to do something, but consistency is necessary to achieving a Healthy Heart. This is not about showing off, but about showing up - each and every day. Being active, involved, and consistent is a decision. What have you started, then stopped? Was it healthy eating or an active lifestyle? One thing you should not stop is drinking water daily. It is required for your health and wholeness. Reassess where you are with daily water intake, then decide to consistently drink more water. Make it a part of your lifestyle and your goal for a Healthy Heart.

SAY IT - GET IT - DO IT

Day 17: I GET TO

"Whatever you do, do it enthusiastically, as something done for the Lord and not for men, knowing that you will receive the reward of an inheritance from the Lord. You serve the Lord Christ."

Colossians 3:23-24

My wife has the most annoying alarm clock in the world. It will go on and on for an hour, and she can sleep through the whole thing. One morning, after listening to her alarm, for what seemed like a lifetime, I nudged her to get up. I reminded her that she would miss her workout if she didn't get moving. She grunted and said the worst phrase in the English language, "Do I have to?"

Do I have to eat right? Do I have to exercise? Do I have to take care of my body? Do I have to value my spirit man? Do I have to invest into my relationship with Christ? I will tell you today what I told her then, "This is not a 'have to,' this is a 'get to.'"

The journey to health and wholeness is not about what we have to do, it is about what we get to do. I get to journey with Christ each and every day. I get to partner with Him in my dreams, passions, desires, and goals. I get to be healthy. The difference between a "have to" and a "get to" is perspective. Your mindset will determine whether you experience victory or defeat. A "have to" mentality is already defeated. It looks for excuses to quit, to stop. A "get to" mentality is already victorious. It embraces each challenge with possibilities and potential. It is looking to excel and advance.

A truly Healthy Heart never comes from a "have to" mentality, but from a heart that has already decided, no matter what, I "get to!"

"This is not a 'have to,' this is a 'get to.'"

54

Day 17 : I GET TO

SAY IT:

"Today, God, I thank You for the chance and opportunity to serve You, to love You and to partner with You in all I pursue and do. I renew my mind with the supernatural possibilities that are found in You. I raise my expectations as I celebrate the joy of my salvation. Today, I thank You that I get to have a great day."

GET IT:

Being part of a fellowship or a church community is not a "have to" but a "get to." Church attendance is not a requirement for eternal life, but it is a valuable asset to Christian living. It is a privilege that we get to experience today. This challenge is simple: first, find a church, a family, or your tribe, then commit to be all in – no matter what. It is through committed relationships that you can receive, lead and perhaps be the difference that is needed.

DO IT:

Time to stretch yourself, literally. Today's stretch is called the forward bend. Stand a few feet behind a chair. Raise both arms overheard and 'hinge' forward from your hips, keeping your back straight. Hold on to the back of the chair to keep steady for a few seconds, then rise back up to stand straight. Repeat this process, as it increases mobility and blood flow. Always remember to breathe and feel free to add additional stretches on your journey to a Healthy Heart.

SAY IT - GET IT - DO IT

Day 18 : INSTANT GRATIFICATION

"But seek first the kingdom of God and His righteousness,
and all these things will be added to you."
Matthew 6:33

Have I lost all the weight yet? Am I ready to run a marathon? Every time a start a diet, I am looking to see those pounds fall right off. The moment I start running, I expect to be able to go 10 miles. The reality of my progress looks much different than I think it should. We start the process of getting physically fit, wanting instant results. We can do the same thing in our relationship with Christ or our spiritual walk. We press into Christ, wanting instant healing, freedom from anger, deliverance from addictions, or relief for pain. Although God can miraculously heal and deliver, sometimes it can be a process. God loves His children and enjoys the process of journeying through life and growth with them. We are looking for the results, He is all about journey. And, God is often doing so much more in us than the one thing we are looking for.

I found, when God dealt with my anger, He first wanted to heal my identity. The anger was a result of my unhealthy view of who I thought I was. Anger was an external expression of an internal hurt. Similarly, I have tried to lose weight before by running, exercising, lifting weights, all the while not realizing that my eating was killing me. Because of that, my diet had to change before anything else could positively change. But when I began the process of a cleanse (ridding my body of toxins that had collected in my system), it took time for my body to trust that I wasn't going to starve it, but instead feed it nutrients needed to thrive. Healing is a process. Growth is a process. A Healthy Heart requires your being on the journey for the long haul.

Day 18 : INSTANT GRATIFICATION

SAY IT:

"Today I choose to rest in the perfect peace of God. I give Him full permission to work in and through me today. I break off anxiety and fear. I give them no permission in my life. I willingly submit to the process of healing and wholeness. I commit to journeying with Christ as He leads me on the best path to a Healthy Heart. Today is going to be a great day because I am not giving up."

GET IT:

Where have you stopped short? Maybe in a dream or passion, schooling, business, or perhaps it is in relationships. Maybe you stopped short of allowing God to truly heal or restore an area in your heart or life. Take a moment, pray, and ask God to reveal areas that you may have stopped short. It is not too late. Invite Him now to partner with you in completing the good work that was begun in your life. Today can choose to join with Him as you journey to a Healthy Heart.

DO IT:

You have tried to eat healthy before and quit. Either it didn't work, or you didn't get the results you wanted as quickly as you wanted them. Healthy eating always takes time. It is not instant. The whole goal of "fast food" is instant gratification. There is value in taking time to cook a proper meal. Fueling your body with healthy, real food makes a statement to you that you are worth the time and nutritional investment. Starting today, for the rest of this Healthy Heart devotional, make a decision for No More Fast Food.

SAY IT - GET IT - DO IT

Day 19 : PROGRESS

*"Let us not become weary in doing good, for at the
proper time we will reap a harvest if we do not give up."*

Galatians 6:9

"Are we there yet?" We have all heard those words before, and most of us have said them a time or two. On my last road trip, my kids asked that question over and over again. Eight hours in the car with them asking, "Are we there yet?" was enough to drive me crazy. It took my son finally asking a different question to change everything. He asked, "How far have we gone?" What my son really wanted to know was whether or not we were making progress.

In life we struggle with the same question: have we have reached our goal yet? Often, that goal can mean the perfect weight, perfect dress size, or being free from addiction. The better questions are, "Have we made any progress?" Have we advanced at all? I am all for being addiction free or finally reaching the goal weight, but not as all or nothing. Measuring success on goal achievement alone greatly discounts the process, where progress is gained and found.

We must not abandon progress in the pursuit of perfection – both in our physical and spiritual walks. In the striving for perfect, we lose the ability to be present in the process, then wonder why we are so tired and empty on the inside. The journey matters. Living your life matters – even in the messy process. Abundant life is not about getting it all right 100% of the time, but about being present for the process and celebrating the progress.

Don't stop now, you have come too far, in your walk with God, and in your journey to a Healthy Heart. Choose today to push forward in Christ, and to celebrate your progress.

> ## "Don't stop now..."

58

Day 19 : PROGRESS

SAY IT:

"Today, God, I celebrate all that You are doing in my life, my family, my dreams and my destiny. I thank You for the victory that I am walking in. I break off doubt that would try to discourage me, weariness that would try to hinder me and fear that would try to stop me. I press into the high calling on my life and I run the race set before me with confidence and boldness. Today is going to be a great day as I progress in greatness!"

GET IT:

: Freedom from fear is a process. It doesn't happen once then is over forever, but it develops every time we choose to trust in each area of our life. You may have learned to trust God in your finances, but still struggle to trust God in others areas, such as relationships. Or, you may trust God in restoring your relationship with your parents, but still struggle with trust in friendships. Breakthrough, freedom, and victory are processes that happen as we advance with Christ in our life. Where are you struggling with fear or trust today? How can you learn to trust God in those areas? Ask God to show you ways that you can learn to trust Him as you progress to a Healthy Heart.

DO IT:

It's a good thing Leg Day only comes once a week. The soreness you feel in your legs the next day shows the progress of growth. Today we will be doing some squats. The squat is one of the best exercises for building lower body strength. Keep your back straight and your chest and shoulders up. Feet set shoulder length apart. Keep looking straight ahead at a spot on the wall. As you squat down, focus on keeping your knees in line with your feet. Lower yourself so your thighs are as parallel to the floor as possible, with your knees over your ankles. Press your weight back into your heels. Keep your body tight, and push through your heels to bring yourself back to the starting position.

SAY IT - GET IT - DO IT

Day 20 : THE POWER OF RESISTANCE

"Finally, be strong in the Lord and in the strength of His might."
Ephesians 6:10

When you go to the gym you are guaranteed to see strong, buff, bulked-up men and women walking around. You can hear their grunts from all over the room, as they lift weights and slam them to the ground. You can watch veins popping, muscles bulging, and sweat dripping as they push their bodies. I was shocked to see one of the stronger guys in the gym working out in front of a mirror with a bright, pink, rubber band. How odd, to see this giant of a man working with this flimsy band, and struggling with each movement he made. So I did what I normally do - I approached the guy and asked him about his workout.

First, he said he was helping his mother get fit. When I turned I saw a sweet, shorter lady standing next to him. Next, he said he started weight training with resistance bands. Resistance bands? Not bench press, not curls, not dead lifts, but resistance bands. The reality is all these forms of weight training are resistance training, which challenges the muscle you are working to overcome the resistance force. As you do this repeatedly, your muscles grow and you get stronger. Strength comes from resistance training in the not backing down, not giving up, not quitting, but instead pressing through and overcoming. Sounds like Christian living.

As Christians, some of us are in resistance training. We continue to face the same obstacle over and over: anger, fear, or depression. It is in the overcoming that we grow stronger. While we are waiting for Christ to move the mountains for us, He is giving us the strength to climb them. In that strength, faith and belief we can speak to mountains and see them moved. Maybe, just maybe, the thing in front of you can make you stronger; if you are willing to face it, with Christ, and overcome. A Healthy Heart comes from being willing to grow stronger.

Day 20 : THE POWER OF RESISTANCE

SAY IT:

"Today, God, I am willing to face what is before me, knowing that You have equipped me with everything I need to walk in victory, confidence and greatness. I refuse to allow lies to discourage me, doubt to derail me, or fear to hold me back. I am pressing on toward the calling on my life and laying hold of the dreams and destiny that You have placed in me. Today is going to be a great day because, in You, I can walk in greatness."

GET IT:

We have talked about forgiveness, its importance and power in your life. We often look at it as a one-time act, a prayer or a statement. For many of us, the true process of forgiveness is something we must do over and over again. There can be resistance, like in strength training, where we forgive but then that grudge, hurt, or fear comes and pushes back. Every time you choose forgiveness you get a little stronger. Today, search your heart, be transparent with God, and choose to face that hurt. Be honest about the pain, then choose to forgive. You will be stronger for it, which is a key to a Healthy Heart.

DO IT:

Not all strength or resistance training requires weights or bands. A push up is resistance training. There is an easier one to do, yet it is still as powerful, the Plank. The Plank is simple, can be done by anyone and it can be done almost anywhere. Get in the pushup position. (Don't worry, you are not doing a pushup.) Put your forearms on the ground parallel to the body, shoulder width apart. Create a straight, strong line from head to toes – a plank, if you will. Hold the position as long as you can (at least 30 seconds). Then rest and try it again.

SAY IT - GET IT - DO IT

Day 21 : PEACE

"Cast all your anxiety on Him for He cares for you."
1 Peter 5:7

Have you ever been in that place where panic begins to wash over you like a giant wave? Your heart begins to pound in your chest like a massive warning signal that will not stop. Your knees get weak and shaky, your stomach gets twisted in a knot, and your palms get wet and sweaty. Your body is responding to the threat of danger. You feel you are losing control, the room is spinning, and all you really want to do is make it all stop. That is called anxiety.

Anxiety is a health killer: physically, mentally and spiritually. Anxiety affects sleep, ability to focus or think clearly, and your actions and reactions. When anxiety has power in your life, it begins to control your decisions and feelings. Once anxiety has permission to rule you, you will begin to look to it for answers in your life. As Christians this is a challenge, because the Lord is supposed to guide us and direct our steps. Despite wind and waves, we are supposed to be rooted and grounded on the solid rock of Jesus. Yet, many have become accustomed to living and partnering with anxiety, and maybe even given it Jesus' place in our hearts.

I am not saying anxiety is not real. God gets it; He knows that anxiety happens, and how large it can feel. That is why He challenges us to give it to Him, rather than take it on ourselves. First Peter encourages you to "Cast all your anxiety on Him..." Choosing to give God your anxiety, your fears, and your worries is a choice you get to make. The beautiful thing is, God doesn't just take your anxiety, He replaces it with perfect peace. His is the peace that surpasses understanding. A Healthy Heart comes from pressing into God's peace.

Day 21 : PEACE

SAY IT:

"Today, God, I break any hold of anxiety, fear, doubt, worry or unbelief. I come out of agreement with their lies and I press into Your truth. I give You my anxieties and my fears. Instead, I choose to lay hold of Your peace in my life. I welcome Your peace to guide me, lead me, encourage me, and lift me up. Today is going to be a great day as I press into Your greatness."

GET IT:

Have you had that panic attack? That anxiety attack that shuts you down or keeps you awake? What is the root of that fear? Take a moment and ask God to reveal it to you, then write it down. Once you know what it is, acknowledge it and give it to God. In exchange, receive His peace in your life and in the situation.

DO IT:

Learning to rest is another key to a Healthy Heart. A key to that rest and relaxation is proper breathing. Most days you have been given a physical challenge for your body. Today the challenge is a breathing exercise. Start by taking a deep breath in through your nose, while counting to four in your head. Then exhale, four seconds, through the nose. Do this slowly three times as you allow your body to rest.

SAY IT - GET IT - DO IT

Day 22 : STEPPING OUT

"'Lord, if it's You,' Peter replied, 'tell me to come to You on the water.'"
Matthew 14:28

Each of my children is very different. When they were younger, my daughter, Meaghan, was quieter and shy, while Brigha was always a little louder and outgoing. When I was teaching the children to swim, I remember placing Brigha on a step in the pool, then calling to her to swim towards me. She never would. She would sit on that step and refuse. I would pick her up, help her paddle around the pool, then sit her back on the step and encourage her to swim to me. Nope, she wanted me to hold her every time. She needed that confidence, that assurance.

My son, Evan, on the other hand, couldn't be kept on the step. During one swim lesson, the teacher placed him on the step to work with another child. The moment she turned around, Evan was off the step trying to swim. Since it was only his second try he sunk straight to the bottom. I had to rescue him, jumping into the pool clothing and all. In my relationship with God, I go back and forth between these two extremes. One moment I want God to just hold me through the waters of life, but when He sets me down and encourages me to venture out, I simply refuse to move. Arms crossed and face stubborn, I sit there until He picks me up again. Other times in my life I don't wait for God at all. I am off on my own, trying my best, risking my all, but sinking. That is, until God picks me up again.

God wants us somewhere in between: close enough where we keep our eyes on Him and journey with Him, but confident enough to step out knowing who we are in Christ, with Christ. The place of a Healthy Heart is found in journeying with Christ, together.

64

Day 22 : STEPPING OUT

SAY IT:

"Today, God, I am excited to journey with You. I will keep my eyes focused on You and who You are in my life, my relationship, my dreams and my passions. Today I will step out boldly, with confidence, into what You have called me to and into the truth of who You say I am. Today will be a great day because today I am partnered with greatness."

GET IT:

Often times God is longing to do a work in our lives, but in our stubbornness we refuse to move, or to allow Him to move in and through us. What has God called you to do or be that you have refused to get off the step and move toward? Perhaps it is a restoration of relationship, reaching out to your neighbor, or being loving in your work place? Today, when you make that decision to partner with God in one of these areas and step out, you are on your way to a Healthy Heart.

DO IT:

Move Day. How is our "moving" coming along? Did you know whenever you walk or run, when you move your arms, you burn more calories? Today as you move, try working your arms. Pump your arms while bending them 90 degrees at the elbows and keeping them close to your body. This will increase the cardiovascular benefit of your activity and improve your Healthy Heart.

Day 23 : REFRESHING

"Repent, then, and turn to God, so that your sins may
be wiped out, that times of refreshing may come from the Lord."
Acts 3:19

I love watering the plants in our yard and garden. It gives me a chance to relax, think, and reflect on my day, without much distraction. I know that watering plants (giving them a cool drink) on a hot day refreshes them. Sometimes when I water, the hose gets kinked, and it stops the whole process. Nothing comes out. It doesn't matter how much I hold the hose, if I don't fix the kink in the line, nothing happens. If nothing flows out, the plants don't get refreshed.

This can happen in our personal lives. We long for refreshing from Holy Spirit. We are doing the work that God has placed on our hearts: loving our family, being faithful at our job, pursuing our passions or dreams. But when we get tired and frustrated, our grace runs low, our patience runs out, and we begin to experience a kink in the flow of Holy Spirit refreshing.

Some people call this burnout. Yet the Bible says we can run and not grow weary. How can this happen? Sometimes we have to unkink the line of refreshing that God is pouring out. Acts 3:19 says, "repent...so refreshing may come." Repenting isn't just that transaction you see at an altar call with people crying. Repenting is about getting in right relationship with God; getting into alignment with Him. It means to have an about face, to turn completely from whatever is distracting you from God and give Him your focus. Your distraction isn't necessarily sinful. It isn't just sin that kinks your line of refreshing. It is anything that pulls you away from intimacy with your Heavenly Father. Today is a good day to repent, press into God and experience His refreshing. A refreshed heart is a Healthy Heart.

Day 23 : REFRESHING

SAY IT:

"Today, God, I let go of anything that is holding me back from pressing into the more of You. I will keep my eyes on You as You direct my path and lead me. I receive Your refreshing in my life as You restore grace, mercy, peace and new levels of love in my life. Today is going to be a great day as I refresh in You."

GET IT:

What is distracting you from pressing into more of God? What is stealing your time, energy and heart away from what matters most? Is there any area in your life from which you need to repent? Make the decision today to repent, turn towards God, and lay hold of Him as He refreshes you with living water.

DO IT:

Water is a key ingredient for a Healthy Heart. Did you know that drinking water can make you eat less, feel full quicker and make you less hungry? It is true. The challenge is to always drink water first, before you eat or grab that snack. Next time you are hungry and you reach for a snack, drink a full glass of water first. That will lead you to a truly Healthy Heart.

SAY IT - GET IT - DO IT

Day 24 : BALANCE

"Because of the Lord's great love we are not consumed, for His compassions never fail. They are new every morning; great is Your faithfulness."
Lamentations 3:22 -23

Like a rollercoaster that doesn't end, we can move between feeling good and feeling bad. Happy then sad. I don't know if you have ever gone through this range of emotions, but I have. I find myself acting then reacting, over and over again.

God is the same yesterday, today and forever. His promises are true; they are "yes" and "amen" (2 Corinthians 1:20). We can count on Him, trust in Him, and rely on Him. As a child of God, our lives are not meant to be a rollercoaster of emotion. Emotions are great! In fact, God gave them to us. But balance is important to victorious Christian living. We are to reflect the character of the God we serve, and He is balanced.

We can get out of balance if we are overreacting to situations we cannot control. In health, I have seen people overreact to their weight by starving themselves. Instead of solving the challenge, overreactions create a whole new set of problems. This can happen in our personal and spiritual life as well. In an effort to contain the chaos of life -managing deadlines, getting kids to school, packing lunches, doing the laundry, etc.- we jump head first one direction, then the next. This creates new chaos. Imbalance.

As a Christian, our balance in life can only come through intimacy with God. The closer we are to Him, the more we understand and trust that He is in control. We will all experience storms of life that toss us to and fro, but we serve a God who can silence those storms. Instead of reacting every time the waves start, we get to remember we are journeying this life with Christ. Pursue balance and, through balance, experience a Healthy Heart.

> **"...balance in life can only come through intimacy with God. "**

68

Day 24 : BALANCE

SAY IT:

"Today, Lord, I draw closer to You. I break off the chaos of emotions that would like to control me, and I submit them to You. Let Your peace surpass my understanding, let Your joy be my strength, let Your kindness lead me and let Your love guide me. Today I rest in the knowledge that You hold all things in Your hand. Today is going to be a great day, because You made today for me."

GET IT:

What are you doing today to cultivate intimacy with God? Praise and worship are invitations for encounters with Christ. You don't have to wait for a worship service to praise God, or to worship Him. You can stop right now, wherever you are, and give Him praise. Take time today, throughout the day, to worship God, whether you are in your home, workplace, or school. Cultivating intimacy with God creates a healthy balance in your life.

DO IT:

Balance in physical training is a key component to a Healthy Heart. It is about physical control. There are many ways to develop strength and balance in your body. One way is to increase core strength through balance. Today, take time to stand on one leg, eyes closed, for 30 seconds. Once finished, switch legs and hold it again for 30 seconds. Do this for a total of five minutes a day and you will see an increase in your physical balance.

Day 25 : SURRENDER

"Peter began to say to Him, 'Behold, we have left everything and followed You."
Mark 10:28

When Peter made the bold statement to Christ that they had left all they had to follow Him, he wasn't just saying that they did it once. It was still true, still happening at that very moment. The life of surrender they chose was still very much active. We can get caught in the mindset that surrender was something we did once, when we gave our life to Christ. True surrender to Christ is an ongoing process, a decision we make every day.

True surrender is that place where we are willing to give Him all areas of our life: eating, attitude, habits, addictions, relationships, and lifestyle. In the surrender, we give Him permission to affect our eternity, not just our current day.

I once saw a guy riding a bicycle while smoking a cigarette. I thought how foolish he looked. God convicted me right then. He began to reveal to me times I have looked that foolish: preaching about love while withholding forgiveness; ministering about grace, yet reserving judgment; times in my life when I stepped out in faith, then tried to accomplish it all on my own, in my own power and strength. During those times, I was frustrated because the results were not what I was expecting. God showed me the frustration was with me because I wasn't willing to truly surrender and give Him everything, holding nothing back.

You may be trying to get physically healthy, but not truly surrendering to the process. Exercising during the day, while eating pizza and ice cream at night, wondering where the results are. That may sound funny, but we really do this in our life. Today, choose to completely surrender to God, both spiritually and physically, and grow in your Healthy Heart.

Day 25 : SURRENDER

SAY IT:

"Today, God, I give You all of me, I hold nothing back. I give You permission to lead me and guide me, to direct my steps and order my path. I surrender to Your will in my life so my life will be a testimony to the goodness of a great God. Today is going to be a great day because I surrender to Your greatness."

GET IT:

What are you still holding onto that you need to give to God? Is it your finances, your workplace, or perhaps your pain or how others have hurt you? Take a moment to write down some of the things you may be struggling with, or holding on to that you know you need to surrender to God. Make a decision today to surrender those things and give Him complete control.

DO IT:

There is a difference between being hungry and being full. Also, hunger and appetite are not the same. Hunger is the need for food, appetite is the desire for food. Eating to feel full is a conditioned response. The best way to curb your appetite is by cutting your hunger. Try eating small, healthy snacks in between breakfast and lunch, and between lunch and dinner. Proteins like almonds, salami, cubed cheese, or vegetables like carrots or celery are good choices. This takes planning and dedication but this act of surrender will help your Healthy Heart.

SAY IT - GET IT - DO IT

Day 26 : I AM ROYALTY

"But you are a chosen people, a royal priesthood, a holy nation, God's special possession, that you may declare the praises of Him who called you out of darkness into his wonderful light."

1 Peter 2:9

There is a story that has been passed down for generations about a King who had a son. The King's son was expelled from the kingdom at infancy and was forced to live in the woods. There he was taken in by a forester who taught him to hunt and fish, know the land, and become a woodsman. At one point, a man from the King's guard discovered the son and returned him to the King. It was there the son discovered he was actually a prince. He was not the pauper that he was brought up to be, but royalty.

As Christians, this is our story as well. Many of us have been brought up in life not realizing that we are royalty, sons and daughters of the King, in God's Kingdom. It wasn't until Jesus rescued me from darkness that I realized I am no longer a pauper in the Kingdom. In the story of the King and the son, the son struggles to live in the truth of his identity - even after learning he is a son of the King. He eats with the servants, not at the royal court. He sleeps with the pigs and not in the Prince's quarters. He was royalty and had access to the Kingdom, but did not know how to live as royalty.

God wants to show and teach you, through your journey and relationship with Him, you are royalty. That may require you to unlearn some old ways and learn to walk in new confidence as a child of the King. You have all Kingdom power and authority at your disposal. God calls you chosen. He calls you son/daughter. He calls you royalty. A Healthy Heart walks fully as a child of the King.

> ## "A Healthy Heart walks fully as a child of the King."

Day 26: I AM ROYALTY

SAY IT:

"I am a child of the King. I am a child of the Most High. I am royalty. Today I break off any thought or mindset that tries to diminish my authority in Christ. I come out of agreement with old ways of the flesh that have held me back, and I walk in victory with Christ. I release the full authority of Heaven in my life and declare that today is going to be a great day."

GET IT:

What do you need to unlearn as a child of the King: fear, doubt, lack? In your upbringing, you may have picked up character traits that are not from your Heavenly Father. Take a moment and write down some of the things that have caused you to struggle. Ask God to teach you His ways. Then, purpose to walk today as a child of the King.

DO IT:

Leg Day couldn't have come any sooner. Today we revisit the classic lunge. Always remember to breathe. Keep your upper body straight, your shoulders back and relaxed, with your chin up. Pick a point to stare at in front of you so you don't keep looking down. Step forward with one leg, lowering your hips until both knees are bent at about a 90-degree angle. Bring that leg back to original position, then switch legs.

SAY IT - GET IT - DO IT

Day 27 : GIVE HIM PRAISE

"Finally, brothers and sisters, whatever is true, whatever is noble, whatever is right, whatever is pure, whatever is lovely, whatever is admirable, if anything is excellent or praiseworthy think about such things."

Philippians 4:8

One of my favorite stories in the Bible is about a King named Jehoshaphat. I love it because, as a kid, I always liked saying his name. I also loved it because Jehoshaphat prays one of my favorite prayers. In the midst of an impossible situation, he did something surprising - he praised the Lord. Praise is one of the most simple, yet powerful things we can do as Christians. However, we often relegate it to a Sunday morning church service. 2 Chronicles 20:5-18 says that Jehoshaphat set his face to seek the Lord.

Jehoshaphat took his mind off the impossibilities before him: the dead end, the disaster, the problem. Instead, he placed his eyes on the only answer. Praise transformed his thinking. It reminded him of the goodness and the greatness of his God.

Praise invites the presence of God to invade our situation. Not only does it shift our attention to supernatural possibilities in God, but it creates an atmosphere where His presence resides. Psalms 22 tells us that God inhabits the praises of His people. For Jehoshaphat, praise was the turning point for his victory in battle; it made an impossible situation possible. Praise can have the same power in your life when you choose, through praise, to remind yourself of God's goodness, greatness, and what He has done. When you partner with God's possibilities, you create an atmosphere where He can reside and transform your circumstances, relationships, battles, even finances. Praise is an important key to truly living with a Healthy Heart.

Day 27: GIVE HIM PRAISE

SAY IT:

"Today, God, I give You praise and thank You for all you have done and are doing in my life. I praise You for Your faithfulness, that Your promises are true, and that You are just. I glorify You for saving me, redeeming me, and restoring me. I know that in You all things are possible. Today, nothing formed against me shall prosper and nothing will hinder me or hold me back. Today is going to be a great day and I praise You for Your greatness."

GET IT:

Remind yourself of what God has done in your life. Take time to praise Him and give Him thanks. What has God done in your life? How has He saved you, in what ways has He redeemed you? Think about it and take time today to set your mind on the things above and give Him praise.

DO IT:

It is Muscle Day, so make sure you are sweating by the time you finish! Work up a sweat. What makes you sweat and what makes me sweat may be different. Some can walk up one flight up stairs and be drenched, for others that would just be a warm up. Whatever you do, make sure you work up a sweat. It will give you a feeling of accomplishment and help you crave the water you need. Sweating helps you release toxins and gets your body doing what it needs to do.

SAY IT - GET IT - DO IT

Day 28 : RESTORATION

"The Lord is my shepherd; I shall not want. He makes me lie down in green pastures. He leads me beside still waters. He restores my soul. He leads me in paths of righteousness for His name's sake."

Psalm 23:1-3

"I need to charge my batteries!" I said that recently after a long week of, well, life. It was more than I thought I could handle. I just felt I needed to charge my internal batteries, so I could do it all again as the next week approached. The reality is, we are seldom given the time or the space to truly recharge. We all have the demands of relationships and responsibilities. If they are not knocking on your door literally, they will knock on your door mentally. It can be hard to detach yourself enough to get sufficient space to recharge. So how do you do it?

In Psalm 23, David talks about the idea that God restores our soul. It literally translates as "He causes life to return." The word "restore" means to "replenish." Your soul is your mind, will, and emotions, and God wants to recharge them all!

Facing exile from a kingdom, a death warrant from a king, and having been anointed to lead a nation, David was in hiding. Yet in the midst of all that, he was not in want - his soul was fully replenished. Through his experience, he shows us how.

The result of his restored soul came from lying in green pastures and walking besides still waters. As a shepherd, David was trying to paint a picture. In verse 2 "green pastures" depicts the lush grass, where sheep would feed and be full. When we feed on God's Word it is life to our spiritual bodies. "He makes me lie down..." There are many times in life when we are not willing to stop long enough to get restored. We serve a Shepherd who will do what needs to be done to get us where we need to be "...beside still waters." These are not waters we are jumping into; they are the still waters of a daily journey. "Beside" reflects our daily connection with God. It is not a once-a-month experience, but an ongoing relationship with Christ. A Healthy Heart comes from being fully recharged in Christ.

Day 28 : RESTORATION

SAY IT:

"Today, God, I press in to your mercy and grace. I allow myself to be renewed in Your Word. I choose to partner with You in my life, relationships, dreams and passions. I break off stress, worry, doubt and fear that would try to hinder me or keep me back. Today is going to be a great day because today I am new in You."

GET IT:

Do you have a favorite scripture - one that brings life to your heart? Take a moment today and meditate on it. If you don't have one, ask God to give one to you. Allow His words to saturate you and release life into your heart. It is in that place of meditating on His Word that faith is built and you are assured of His promises in your life.

DO IT:

I once had a doctor tell me, "I am prescribing you a massage." That sounded great, but I never did it. It can be hard to take time for yourself. So today, do something to pamper you. Get a massage, a manicure, take a long bath, or go on a walk or hike to explore the outdoors. Take some time doing whatever brings you peace. It is time to rest and restore yourself - your Healthy Heart needs it.

SAY IT - GET IT - DO IT

Day 29 : GREATNESS

"For we are God's handiwork, created in Christ Jesus to do good works, which God prepared in advance for us to do."
Ephesians 2:10

Culturally, the idea of greatness has often been reduced to a singular moment or event. "That was a great meal." "We had a great time on vacation." "You were great in that performance." The moment you achieve a great feat, it is done. Then you have to achieve it again. That's a lot of pressure!

Yet when we think of God as being great, we don't think about His greatness as being a one-time event. His greatness is never ending, everlasting, never failing. It's who He is. When greatness isn't something you do, but who you are, everything you do has the potential to be great. I know that every plate of food a great chef puts out is going to be great. Why? Because in knowing their greatness, they refuse to serve anything that is not great. Knowing you are great changes your thinking, your expectation, and your way of living.

Think of this: our Great God, mighty God, victorious God, is living in you! His greatness is in you, therefore you are great. When you shift your mindset to that truth, you will no longer strive for greatness, but live from greatness.

In the gospels, the disciples argue about who is the greatest. Not because of pride or arrogance, but because being in the presence of Christ gave them revelation of their greatness. When you are in the presence of the Most High and are partnered with Him in life, you cannot help but feel great, believe great, and walk in greatness. Christ didn't rebuke them for "greatness" thinking. He simply showed them the way. A Healthy Heart comes from realizing (in Christ) you are great, then walking in the truth of that greatness.

Day 29 : GREATNESS

SAY IT:

"Today, God, I release revelation of Your greatness into my life, my family, my dreams and my desires. I break off any false or wrong thinking that tries to diminish the power of who You are in my life. I choose to partner with You as I press into my calling and I know that today is going to be a great day, because in You I am great."

GET IT:

Through *40 days of a Healthy Heart* we are coming out of agreement with lies you have believed about yourself and coming into agreement with God's truths. Many times we struggle with believing we are great because of lies we have bought into about who we are, our character or ability. Take a moment and think about what untruth you have believed about yourself and ask God what He thinks. A Healthy Heart is birthed out of knowing, in Christ, you are great.

DO IT:

Don't give up! There, I said it. At almost 30 days it is easy to feel like quitting, stopping, caving, compromising. Don't do it. Don't stop. Today is a day to move, walk, run, jog. Get outside and experience some fresh air. Whatever you do, don't quit. A Healthy Heart comes from a lifestyle of choosing to be healthy.

Day 30 : ARTIFICIAL

"How sweet are Thy words unto my taste
Yea, sweeter than honey to my mouth!"
Psalm 119:103

Because I was a chubby kid, I drank a lot of Diet Coke growing up. The words "Zero Calories" enticed me. The reality is that there is nothing that has "zero" influence on our body. People had always tried to scare me away from diet soda with stories of what artificial sweetener could do to me. Those scare tactics never worked. Not until I talked with Sami Kader did I hear something that made sense to me. Sami didn't try to tell me I was poisoning my system or that I was going to die from soda. He simply said, "Matthew, you are doing all this work to be healthy and that diet soda is holding you back. It's artificial - your body doesn't know how to process it. It doesn't know what to do with a fake substitute. It's actually slowing your body down." I learned that Diet Coke becomes a speed bump for my body to process. I may have reduced calorie intake through the soda, but now it could take three times longer for my body to burn the other calories I have ingested.

We can do this spiritually, too. You can reduce God's Word to something that costs you nothing, a zero-calorie gospel that tastes sweet and feels good, but slows down your Christian living. It can be artificial, like a grace that says, "Do whatever you want, it's okay with God." Artificial mercy says, "God does not mind; your bad choices don't grieve His heart." Artificial love is a love that costs nothing, but a love that costs nothing isn't real and doesn't bring life. The Word of God may require something of you: to be active, grow, change, mature, or to sacrifice. But your spirit, soul, and body can process the cost because it is real. Living by the Word of God is life bringing, has nutritional value to your spiritual life, and is sweet to your soul. It is a choice. A Healthy Heart comes from choosing the real deal.

Day 30 : ARTIFICIAL

SAY IT:

"God, your Word is life to my soul, it is refreshing and restoring. I receive the challenge to walk in the fullness of You and of those things You have called me to in my life, relationships and destiny. Today I choose to walk in true love, lay hold of Your authentic mercy, and operate in redeeming grace. I will not substitute greatness; instead I will lay hold of it today and choose to be great."

GET IT:

Where have you substituted one of God's truths for an artificial one? One of the artificial substitutes the world experiences on a regular basis is synthetic love. God has called us to love the world around us with an agape, self-sacrificing, unconditional love. How can you display that kind of love to the world around you today? Choose daily to live the love that Christ has called you to and experience a truly Healthy Heart.

DO IT:

Not everyone is ready to completely eliminate diet soda or artificial sweeteners from their diet. Start with something less drastic, like cutting out diet soda (or fake substitutes) in one area or one time of the day. Kick starting your metabolism takes time. It can be like turning the Titanic: lots of little moves that ultimately cause direction change. It can take up to three months before you truly see a difference, but it is worth it for a Healthy Heart.

SAY IT - GET IT - DO IT

Day 31 : FLEXIBLE

""Nevertheless, I will bring health and healing to it; I will heal my people and will let them enjoy abundant peace and security."

Jeremiah 33:6

When I was a child, my dad preached a sermon in which he said something that has stuck with me for years. I remember the quote because it sounded biblical, but it is not in the Bible. He said, "Blessed are the flexible, for they shall not be broken." In life, I have often found myself to be very inflexible; I don't bend, I simply break. For years I had a standard for living that left me unwilling to bend on rules and regulations. That is great for living in religion, but void of grace for living in relationship. My inability to be flexible was becoming dangerous.

In our physical health, being flexible is an integral part of our wholeness. It is vital to keep from hurting ourselves (or others) as we exercise. Flexibility in our body takes time, purpose and work. It doesn't just happen instantly. It is the same in Christian living. God bestows His grace upon us so that we can live lives that are gracious. We have to choose to receive that grace, choose to live in that grace, then practice that grace.

My inability to be flexible was based on my belief that I had it all figured out. It was rooted in a belief that I knew the best outcome, the best way to act in every situation, and it showcased my inability to be teachable. Inflexibility leaves us unable to grow. Life rarely goes according to plan and I have learned that my way has not always been the best way. I discovered I cannot control the situations I am facing or the lives of those with whom I am journeying. God's grace allows me to remember that God is in control. I still have a lot to learn, and together we can all grow and bend. A Healthy Heart learns to reside in the grace of God.

> ## "Blessed are the flexible, for they shall not be broken."

Day 31 : FLEXIBLE

SAY IT:

"Today, God, I break off the form and function of religion. I press into Your grace and I release it over my life, my family, my workplace, my dreams and my destiny. I release grace over those who think differently, live differently, and work differently than me. I will make an effort to find You in every life and situation I encounter. Today is going to be a great day as I live a life of grace."

GET IT:

The grace of God is His love in action when we deserve it the least. We are called to extend love's grace to those around us when they deserve it the least. In our willingness to bend, we become flexible, even when it is inconvenient. Today, look for ways to extend grace to those around you.

DO IT:

Stretching is a stress reliever. It increases blood flow and oxygen to your muscles. Today take some time to stretch. Try this good and easy stretch. Get in the pushup position. Put one foot over the top of the other and press the heel of your lower foot away from you, toward the floor. Hold that for a few seconds and then switch feet. This stretches your Achilles tendon and your calf.

SAY IT - GET IT - DO IT

Day 32 : HUNGER

"Blessed are those who hunger and thirst for righteousness, for they will be filled."
Matthew 5:6

The English Dictionary contains a relatively new word that often describes me: hangry. It means to be irritable and angry as a result of being hungry. I am not talking about a casual desire for food, just waiting at a restaurant for your order to come, or the agitation you feel while waiting for the preacher to finish so you can get to In-n-Out Burger. I am talking about the aggressive agitation that consumes you when you haven't eaten in (what feels like) days. You cannot think straight, talk straight or walk straight. All you can focus on is getting some food. But even the process of getting the food into you is taking too long and it irritates you. I am talking about being hangry!

What Jesus is talking about is not just a casual hunger for righteousness. One time I was going to get burgers, so I asked my friend if he was hungry. He said, "I guess, if you are going." That is not hungry: that is available. Jesus wants us to be hangry for righteousness; to be consumed with right living with Him. In that place of hunger we experience true, right living with our Heavenly Father. If you only conveniently desire right relationship with God, when it doesn't happen or you are not "filled," you may not be surprised or bothered. God longs for you to desperately desire to be in right standing with Him - so much so that you will let nothing stop you until you get it. That hunger transforms, gets filled, and changes the world. A hungry heart is a Healthy Heart.

Day 32 : HUNGER

SAY IT:

"I desire You, God, in my life today. I desire Your presence, Your spirit, Your leading, and Your counsel in my relationships, work place, family, dreams and my desires. I long to be in greater relationship with You. I invite You to fill me and move through me. Today allow my life to be a testimony to the greatness of a great God."

GET IT:

What are you hungering for? In your spiritual walk with God, are you longing to: draw closer to Christ, know Him more, or allow Him to lead you or guide you? Take time today and pray that God would increase your hunger and desire for Him.

DO IT:

Try this, eat something simple and healthy right when you wake up. Food jump starts your metabolism. Your metabolism is the rate at which your body burns calories. It doesn't matter whether you have a fast or slow metabolism, eating first thing in the morning fuels your body to better metabolize food. You are on your way to a Healthy Heart.

SAY IT - GET IT - DO IT

Day 33 : LET GO

"Let all bitterness and wrath and anger and clamor and slander be put away from you, along with all malice. Be kind to one another, tenderhearted, forgiving one another, as God in Christ forgave you."

Ephesians 4:31-32

I am a pack rat. Well, I used to be a pack rat...and I liked it. I loved holding on to things because I never knew when or where I might need them. It took my wife to break me of this horrible addiction. I call it an addiction because, for me, that is what it was: a compulsive desire to hold onto things.

When Siobhan and I first got married, I remember her asking me what was in a trunk in our garage. I told her it was a few things I had kept from when I was a child. Curious, she opened the case. Inside were all sorts of memorabilia from my childhood, none of them sacred or irreplaceable. It contained old Coke bottles, gum wrappers, baseball cards (of players who no one remembers), stickers that were used and worn...and more. She looked at my chest filled with junk and said, "Let's throw it all away." I was shocked, hurt, and offended. Who did she think she was? These were keepsakes from my childhood. She felt they just took up space.

The reality is she was right. I was holding on just to hold on. I didn't need these things. They just took up space. How many times do we hold onto things (hurt feelings, anger, resentment, fear) that are just taking up space? It could be a childhood memory that neither defines us, nor holds a special place in our heart, but is keeping us back from moving forward and growing in Christ?

Learning to let go is vital for your ability to grow. Letting go does not mean that your experience wasn't real; it just no longer gets to take up space in your life, in your living. Refuse to give it a place. A Healthy Heart is a heart that learns to let go.

Day 33 : LET GO

SAY IT:

"Today, God, I choose to let go of fear, anger, unforgiveness, resentment and hurt. I no longer give place to old mindsets in my life, but renew my mind in You today. I release a fresh portion of Your goodness, joy and mercy in my life. Today is going to be a great day as I let go and pursue the fullness of You."

GET IT:

It took Siobhan to help me get rid of some old things that were taking up space in my life. What is taking up space in your life that is not necessarily bad, but is not good? It could be a friendship, a TV show, an addiction, or a habit that God is saying today is the day to let go. Make a decision to let go and make a change today.

DO IT:

Getting organized and cleaning can be great for our mental health and it can have physical rewards as well. Take some time today to deal with that "junk" drawer, closet or that trunk in your garage. Sort and clear it out. You will feel better and more accomplished for it.

SAY IT - GET IT - DO IT

Day 34 : BREATHE

"Let everything that has breath praise the Lord."
Psalms 150:6

Breathing is essential to life. If you stop breathing, you stop living. On average we take about 26,000 breaths each day. That is a lot of breath! But not all breaths are created equal. Specialists say we only need to breathe 4 to 5 times a minute to receive the optimum energy level from our oxygen. Most of us do much more than that. In fact, most people breathe up to 20 times a minute. We may be breathing, but not taking time to breathe in deep. Shallow, quick breaths expel the good stuff before it ever gets into our system, but deep breaths are the ones that replenish our body and supply sufficient oxygen where we need it.

Regarding breathing, there is bad breath, good breath and God breath. When God created man, He took the dirt and dust of the earth in His hands. He drew it up close towards His face and He breathed into it. That breath created life and potential. God's breath renews, restores and gives purpose. In our Christian walk we can be so busy with the activities of church, events, and programs that we don't take time to breathe in the renewing, life-giving breath of God. Just breathing, functioning, and going through the motions of life is a stark contrast to fully living. God does not want us to just live; He wants us to have abundant life – which requires some deep breaths. Breathe God in and allow Him to revitalize every area of your life, from your relationships to your dreams and passions. Deep breaths renew your soul. It is here, in God's refreshing presence, that you experience a Healthy Heart.

"Deep breaths renew your soul."

88

Day 34 : BREATHE

SAY IT:

"Today, God, I breathe in deeply Your breath of Life. I allow it to fill and replenish every area of my being. Restore me, renew me, refresh me and allow new life to spring up in me. Today I praise You for You are a great God who loves me greatly."

GET IT:

Stop. Just for a moment, stop. Don't get so busy, that you don't take time to breathe in God. Let Him resource you in your pursuit of abundant living. Take a moment today and praise God, meditate on His promises, and allow Him to pour out His goodness in and through you.

DO IT:

Breathing is essential to healthy living. While exercising, proper breathing is necessary for maximum benefit. Take a moment to breathe. Stand straight up with your back against a wall. Slowly inhale through your nose for four seconds then exhale for four seconds, through your nose. Take three deep breaths now, and several times today. Now you are breathing toward a Healthy Heart.

SAY IT - GET IT - DO IT

Day 35 : MOTION EQUALS EMOTION

"Your beginnings will seem humble, so prosperous will your future be."
Job 8:7

When something should be second nature to you, or when you learn something you can never forget, they say "it's like riding a bike." They obviously were not with me when I learned to ride a bike. It wasn't easy, and this was before they made you wear helmets. I had cuts and bruises, scrapes and falls, crashes and more crashes. I sure hope everything isn't like riding a bike. The one thing I did glean from learning to ride a bike is that you have to keep moving. I remember finally getting the motion going. Just then my mother called out to me and as I turned to see her waving at me, I stopped, then fell over. Looking back hinders your ability to move forward, and not moving forward can cause you to stumble and fall.

When I finally got the rhythm of riding a bike, it was amazing. I had the wind in my hair, the feeling of fresh air, the sense that I was alive. That is when I discovered that sitting on a bike is not as much fun as riding a bike. Being stationary on something that was meant to move is no fun at all. We are not stationary beings. We are created for movement and, through that movement there is the feeling of being alive.

I love what Sami Kader says, "Motion equals emotion." When you move, you feel better: alive, vibrant, and healthy. Getting up and moving positions you to feel, see, and experience more abundance in life. You can have dreams and passions, but those require movement. Sitting on them, waiting for them to happen, is like sitting on a bike. It has potential, but no momentum. It requires movement. So do you! A Healthy Heart is a heart on the move.

Day 35 : MOTION EQUALS EMOTION

SAY IT:

"Today, God, I partner with You, in all that I say and do. I allow Your Spirit and presence to move in and through me. I break off fatigue from my relationships, feelings, dreams and destiny. I press into the active presence of Your Spirit. Today is going to be a great day because today we are going places."

GET IT:

Where have you been stationary that God wants you to move in your life? I am not talking about moving to a different country or town. I am talking about taking action: dreams or goals that require you to risk and step out in faith. Today is a good day to start moving toward those dreams.

DO IT:

Get out and move. Don't think that if you cannot run a mile or go to the gym, it's not worth moving at all. Movement matters – all movement. Get out today and move: somewhere, something, somehow, and make it count. It is time to move toward a Healthy Heart.

Day 36 : CONSISTENCY

"Therefore, my beloved brothers, be steadfast, immovable, always abounding in the work of the Lord, knowing that in the Lord your labor is not in vain."
1 Corinthians 15:58

I remember the very first day that I went to the gym. I didn't work out at all. I sat in the parking lot freaked out about going to the gym. I had never been to a gym before. I had no idea what to expect, what it would be like, where to go, or how to use the equipment, so I went home. Sami Kader told me, "Great job. That is the start. Now do it again." I said, "What, sit in the parking lot again?" He replied, "YES! If that is all you can do right now, start there." From the parking lot I worked up the courage to walk inside, use an elliptical machine for 10 minutes, then escape. I did that for a month. From there my confidence grew enough that I went from the elliptical to a treadmill to a stair stepper. I progressed from machines to weights, until one day I ended up in a circuit training class. The goal is consistency. Instead of overwhelming yourself with what you think you have to do, do what you can do - but do it consistently. Keep reasonable expectations. Don't stop, don't give up. Sitting in that parking lot may not have been a workout, but it changed my life. It set me on the road to a Healthy Heart.

Sometimes starting small is all you can do. If all you can do is walk through the doors of a gym, start there, make it a habit then watch how health grows. It is the same with your walk with Christ. You may have journeyed much of your life without inviting God to be a part or involved. Even as a Christian, it is possible to partner with Christ for eternal life, but not for daily living. You can transform that relationship by choosing today to walk, closer with God, inviting Him into your relationships, workplace, or on your morning drive to work. Start, talk to Him. Create a consistent relationship with your Heavenly Father, then watch as it grows. A Healthy Heart happens one day at a time.

Day 36 : CONSISTENCY

SAY IT:

"Today, God, I choose to walk with You, to journey with You, to partner with You, in all I say and do. I break off anything that would try to hinder me from becoming the child of God You have called me to be. I come out of agreement with doubt, stress, and fear and I release the fullness of Your goodness in my life. Today is going to be a great day as I walk in greatness."

GET IT:

Relationships are built with time and intention. Your relationship with God was not meant to only be a one-time prayer, but a relationship built on your daily journey with Him in life and living. Your prayer time does not have to be long, but it does have to be intentional. Choose today to take time and talk with God. Then choose to do it daily and see how your Healthy Heart in Christ grows.

DO IT:

You may have already started eating healthier, so don't stop. Allow your decision to pursue health to grow you. Each day, stay consistent with healthy choices in what you eat, drink and how you move. Health is not a one-day decision to lose weight, eat better, or exercise more, but a day-to-day decision to believe that you matter. Today's challenge: don't stop, stay consistent, and have a Healthy Heart.

SAY IT - GET IT - DO IT

Day 37 : GET UNCOMFORTABLE

"For God has not given us a spirit of fear, but of power and of love and of a sound mind."

2 Timothy 1:7

My wife wanted to make some room in our garage, so she asked if she could get rid of a few items. These were unused things that had sat in our garage for a long time. One of the biggest pieces was a large exercise bike. Next to it was an old treadmill. I began to look around at all sorts of fitness equipment that I had accumulated: a stair stepper, dumbbells, two weight benches, free weights, fitness bands, a medicine ball, and ab (abdominal) roller - all just sitting, waiting to be used. Working out at home can be hard. You can have all the right equipment and availability, and still never get it done. There is something motivating about getting out of your comfort zone and making time and space outside of your normal routine to get healthy. When I go to the gym, go running outdoors, or workout with a friend or trainer, an hour and a half can go by so fast I don't even know it. When I am inside at my home, I am watching every minute.

It is the same with spiritual exercise. In our homes we can worship, pray, and fellowship. But there is something powerful about getting out of the house and coming together in a fellowship, a church, and worshiping. Not everyone is comfortable with public worship: people lifting their hands, maybe dancers or worshippers with flags. Change is usually uncomfortable. It may challenge you, but it is still powerful. Getting out of your comfort zone in any area of your life can help you press deeper in to Christ. When you choose to pursue a Healthy Heart, you have to make change (physical and spiritual) which requires a willingness to be uncomfortable. Getting uncomfortable with where you are can lead you on the path to a Healthy Heart.

"Change is usually uncomfortable."

Day 37 : GET UNCOMFORTABLE

SAY IT:

"Today, God, I break of the complacency that keeps me where I am and holds me back from my destiny and dreams. I break off feelings of inconvenience or apathy and I press into the greatness that lies before me. I release the fullness of your strength, goodness and power in my life. I know that today is going to be a great day!"

GET IT:

Step out of your comfort zone. Many people struggle with praying out loud; just hearing the sound of their voice bothers them. Try it today, pray out loud, where you can hear yourself. It doesn't have to be with a group of people. Pray, out loud. It will build your spirit, ignite your faith, and stir your heart. That is healthy.

DO IT:

Get out of your home. If you have been exercising or working out at home, challenge yourself today to get outside. Go check out a gym, walk around the block, run in the park or workout with a friend, but get uncomfortable. Try a new exercise, a new stretch, a new breathing exercise and challenge yourself to get uncomfortable.

SAY IT - GET IT - DO IT

Day 38 : THE POWER OF "NO"

"Let what you say be simply 'Yes' or 'No'..."
Matthew 5:37

The cleanse I was on was filled with a list of things that I could and could not eat and drink. Some of them were simple for me, like no soda. Other items were much harder: no bread, no wheat, and no rice. During this cleanse I ordered a salad, in an attempt to be healthy. When it was served it was filled with large, glorious, beautiful croutons. In the world of croutons, these croutons were king. I stared at delicious croutons for what felt like hours. It was in that moment I discovered an element of strength I didn't know was there. Slowly, methodically, I removed those croutons, one at a time, and set them on the edge of my plate. As the waiter saw what I was doing he said, "I could get the kitchen to remove the croutons for you." "No!" I exclaimed. There was something powerful in my removing those croutons, something victorious in the ability to say "NO." Sure, I could have gotten croutons removed. For me, the big question is: when life happens, will I have the ability to say no for myself?

I had someone tell me once that life would be great if nothing bad ever happened. Probably true, but Jesus assured us that in this life we will have tribulation. Tribulation, covered in glorious croutons! However, just because you were given a "crouton" doesn't mean you have to keep it. Whether your crouton is fear, doubt, loneliness, depression, or anything else, you do not have to accept it. Some days are going to be a struggle, but God gave you strength, love, self control, and the ability to say "NO." Since that day, I always get my salad with croutons, and I love taking them off. There is something powerful in knowing I don't have to eat them. A Healthy Heart comes from the ability to say "no" to unhealthy situations.

Day 38 : THE POWER OF "NO"

SAY IT:
"Today, God, I say yes to You, Your will, Your grace and Your mercy in my life. I say no to the lies of the enemy that would try to hinder or diminish me. I say no to unhealthy thoughts that would try to bring me down. I stand firm on Your promises and your Word. Today is going to be a great day as I choose today to have a Healthy Heart."

GET IT:
Just because you "feel" something, does not mean it's correct, true, or that it has to have power in your life. Our feelings are not always right. Our feelings are often dictated by our circumstances, and our circumstances can be tossed to and fro like a ship on a stormy sea. Where have your feelings not been lining up with what God says about you, your circumstances or your destiny? Choose today to lay hold of His Word and say "NO" to anything that is not from Him.

DO IT:
Remove the crouton! Well, maybe croutons are not your problem. It may be ice cream, sweets, sugary drinks, or coffee. You know what your crouton is. Today, choose to say "NO" and remove it, cut it out of your life - if only for a day. You are on your way to a Healthy Heart.

Day 39 : JUST THE BEGINNING

"Commit your actions to the Lord, and your plans will succeed."
Proverbs 16:3

"I did it! I ate a salad and now I am healthy." I said those words, tongue in cheek, as Sami Kader shook his head. That is how I felt, though. I made one decision for health and now felt I had achieved health. That meant I could go back to eating pizza, hamburgers and drinking diet soda. We all know how silly that sounds. The truth is, health is not a one-time decision to eat healthy. Sustained health is not just a diet plan; it has to be more than just a 40 day plan. Health is a lifestyle. It is making the decision that "you matter." A Healthy Heart is about choosing to value you always, everyday, in every circumstance. Health didn't start just because you picked up a book, nor should it end after Day 40. A healthy life begins with an initial decision, followed by committing to that decision daily. It is the same way with your Christian walk.

Salvation is powerful. It is the gateway to personal relationship and intimacy with Christ. It assures us eternal life, and it is the path to victorious living. Salvation restores us, redeems us, renews us, and releases faith, hope, and belief. Yet salvation is more than one prayer we prayed when we first accepted Jesus. Salvation is a process, a day by day journey. In Philippians, Paul tells us to work out our Salvation. Salvation is a decision we make, every day. When we believe in our heart and confess with our mouths that Christ is Lord, we are at the starting line of this journey, not the finish line. It is the beginning of a Healthy Heart. Every day we choose relationship with Jesus, value ourselves, and learn to love ourselves like Christ loves us, we choose a Healthy Heart. It is from that place of relationship, love and health we impact the world and see transformation take place around us. A Healthy Heart happens every day that you choose to be healthy.

Day 39 : JUST THE BEGINNING

SAY IT:

"I commit today to You, Lord, and choose to walk in relationship with You. I receive Your truth that I am a child of the Most High, called, chosen, and highly favored. I break off any lie that would try to diminish who I am in Christ. Today is going to be a great day as I am walking in Your greatness."

GET IT:

Physical health takes a plan, preparation, determination and a daily decision. Spiritual health requires the same commitment: choosing to forgive and live forgiven; to love and live loved; deciding daily to walk in relationship with Christ. In what area of spiritual health is Christ challenging you to grow? What can you do daily to commit to that healthy lifestyle?

DO IT:

What changes have you made in your life physically that have been for the better during this Healthy Heart devotional? Was it to move more, drink more water, or cut out unhealthy foods or chemical substitutes? What changes are you willing to commit to as ongoing lifestyle for a Healthy Heart?

SAY IT - GET IT - DO IT

Day 40 : FINISH STRONG

"I have fought the good fight, I have finished the race, I have kept the faith."

2 Timothy 4:7

Imagine if when you first got saved you already loved like you do now. What if you had mature grace and mercy, forgiveness and joy, strong faith and great belief? In your journey with Christ you have grown and learned. Even so, you still may not do everything correctly all of the time. I don't always love like I know I should, but I know a lot more about what love is than I did when I first received Christ.

In the same way, imagine if you started 40 days to a Healthy Heart already drinking water like you should, or moving more. What if you began having already cut out junk food or unhealthy drinks right at the start. Imagine how far you would be now.

That is why having Healthy Heart isn't something simply *achieved*, as much as it is journeyed and *lived*. Every day gives you the opportunity to learn, grow, develop, and get better, stronger, and healthier. One of the pastors on our team, Kristine Dohner, always says, "When you know better, you do better." Health is the journey of knowing better, then doing better.

You began *40 Days to a Healthy Heart* learning that you are valuable. As you end this devotional my hope is that there is even more that you love and value about yourself. It is important that you know that you are worth it. The more you value you, the more that you will take care of yourself. This is not the end of your quest for health, but the beginning of a Healthy Heart.

"This is not the end, but the beginning of a Healthy Heart."

Day 40 : FINISH STRONG

SAY IT:

"I thank You, God, that I am fearfully and wonderfully made. I thank You that today You have equipped me with all the resources to walk in victory and my life can be a testimony to the greatness of a good God. Today I will not back off or back down from the calling that You have on my life and I choose today to walk in wholeness in You. Today I choose a Healthy Heart."

GET IT:

"I love you." Those three words sealed my wedding vows to my wife on the day we got married. I have chosen to say them every day since. If I just said them once and expected her to "just know" from then on, our relationship would have suffered. Many of us love God and expect Him just to know. Choose today to express your love for Him and choose not to stop. With a Healthy Heart, every day matters.

DO IT:

Push through, finish strong, don't quit! I hear these words yelled while lifting weights, running marathons, and in circuit training. When you finish strong you set yourself up to start strong. Over the past 40 days you have set yourself up to start strong. Today isn't the end of healthy living, but the start of a healthy lifestyle. Today, see what you can do all together: moving, eating right, drinking water, breathing right, stretching. Challenge yourself to finish strong and live life with a Healthy Heart.

About Sami

At age eight, Sami Kader started to gain weight and began to face rejection from those around him. Throughout his elementary, junior high and early high school years, he was mocked, bullied, and generally unaccepted by his peers. At age 16, and his highest weight of 300 pounds, a family friend intervened and insisted that Sami join him on his daily trips to the gym. By age 18, he had lost over 100 pounds and landed a job at a nationwide chain of health clubs.

Now a full time youth motivational speaker, Sami has received local and national media attention for his work with the youth in his community.

Sami believes that all children deserve the chance to succeed, and that believing in yourself is one of the most important parts of leading a happy, healthy life. To find out more about Sami, visit his website www.samikader.com

Made in the USA
Columbia, SC
17 June 2017